Listening to

The Challenges

A Devotional Commentary

On the New Testament

Letter of James

James A. Prette

Contents

Introduction

LISTENING

It is my conviction that the point of all existence is to glorify God. All of creation exists to reflect the experience of God. Our purpose as human beings is to know, love, and serve God and enjoy God forever.[1] We get to be in dynamic relationship with the Living God, and we get to grow in that relationship. We are invited into a transformative journey. It is an invitation to grow in wisdom and maturity, that we might become the servant-friends of God whom, God is shaping as a Church and a future "bride". Towards that purpose, God invites us to listen to His[2] Word, to be instructed and changed by His inspiring revelation. This is why Christians gather

---

[1] This is my addition to the answer to the first question in the 'Shorter Catechism' of the 'Westminster Confession' 1647 (Q: *"What is the chief end of man?"* – A: *"Man's chief end is to glorify God and enjoy Him forever"*).

[2] I will be using the grammatically correct, English, gender-neutral pronouns for God throughout this book, though the words are tragically also male gender specific. I wish I had adequate proper English words to differentiate the non-gendered, eternal God from my offensively male dominated language. Here is Marva Dawn's apology for this situation, with which I completely agree: *"Out of my concern to reach the widest audience possible, I have chosen to refer to God with the pronouns **he, his**, and **him**, which I have always understood as gender-neutral — and yet personal — when used in connection with God. I apologize to anyone who might be offended by my word choices and pray that you will accept my decision to use our inadequate language as carefully as possible to speak to the widest audience. Certainly God is neither masculine nor feminine, but more than all our words can ever connote"*. Marva J. Dawn, A *Royal Waste of Time: The Splendor of Worshiping God and Being Church for the World, Belongs* (Grand Rapids: Wm. B. Eerdmans Publishing Co., 1999), 1.

on Sundays. We gather to worship. We gather to be changed by God. We gather to listen to the Word of God - read, sung, prayed, and preached, that we might be transformed, that we might be molded into the kinds of Spiritual people God wants us all to be. As followers of Christ, we also get to grow in developing personal habits of listening to God Word. That's why we endeavor to always look to God's texts, to what God has revealed to us through his Scriptures, and to study these texts together. And so I am inviting you to join me in this study of the little letter of 'James' in the New Testament. It is my hope, above anything else, that you may hear God speak to you through this study of this part of His Word.

The translation of 'James' I am using is my own, developed through the study of the Greek text (Novum Testamentum Graece) for the expositional teaching of this letter that I have had the privilege to do in many settings over 40 years. I will quote from the 2011 New International Version (NIV) through out the body of the commentary because this is the most commonly used translation amongst my acquaintances. I will walk through the whole of James' letter to listen to the entire message. I will invite you to listen to every word; stopping at some interesting parts (according to me!), asking questions, considering what it might mean for us. Please consider this a friendly conversation between God (through His friend, James), me (a friendly guide who happens to also be named, James), and you. I hope these will be a series of friendly, yet challenging chats, as we "listen" to God's Word through James together. It is my conviction that the act of listening to the text, and letting it speak God's message to us is the important task of followers of Jesus. I have done a lot of homework on these texts, but I am only a fellow listener. I am continuing to listen to these texts, and I invite you to join me on this journey of listening to what God may be saying to us. I am calling our studies "a devotional commentary". I mean for this to be an expositional commentary of the whole of James' message, and that it will lead to a deeper, richer devotion to God in our hearts and actions.

INVITATION TO PERSEVERANCE

In studying the letter of 'James', a theme about what James is doing emerged for me. I believe the whole message of the letter hinges on what he says at the beginning of his letter. In 1:3,4 he shares his concern that followers of Christ would continue in the invitation to persevere in growing more deeply in knowing, loving, and serving Jesus. James hoped his friends would persevere in that invitation. It's that perseverance that will help one to grow in the wisdom and maturity God calls us in to, and to become more and more an instrument of God's love and justice in His world. And that's God's goal for us all - that we would grow up in wisdom and maturity. God uses the trials, troubles, and tribulations of this life as a means strengthen our faith and build the kind of perseverance in us that deepens wisdom and maturity. So that's the theme. There are many life experiences that are constantly challenging the maturity of one's faith and calling one to greater perseverance. Each chapter will explore a different life challenge that James addresses.

INVITATION TO ITIMACY

Paula D'Arcy said, "*God comes to us disguised as our life*".[3] All of creation is continually revealing God (Psalm 19, Rom. 1:19, 20). Our lives are a part of that revealing creation. So, in paying attention to what we are experiencing in the challenges of our daily lives we may pay attention to God in our lives. These challenges are not a matter of toughing it out through the tests, trials and temptations we face. Rather, each challenge is an invitation to intimately meet with God more deeply, to meet God in the failing of tests, to meet God in the refining trials, to meet God in the midst of temptations, and to meet God in all the challenges to our faith. The psalmist wrote, "*Deep calls to deep*" (Ps. 42:7). God is calling us into a deep relationship with Him and into deep growth in personal wisdom and maturity. All of life is meant to draw us more deeply into relating to God; to draw us into paying attention to God in the very center of our lives. A.W. Tozer wrote, "*God dwells in His creation and is everywhere indivisibly present in all His works. This is boldly taught by prophet and apostle and is accepted by Christian theology generally. That is, it appears in the books, but for some reason it has not sunk into the average Christian's heart so as to*

---

[3] Quoted by Richard Rohr, *Everything Belongs* (New York: Crossroad Publishing, 2002), 130.

become a part of his believing self. Christian teachers shy away from its full implications, and, if they mention it at all, mute it down till it has little meaning"[4]. Let's not "mute" the voice of God revealing what He wants us to deeply experience of Him through our experiences in His creation. Fredrick Buechner wrote, "*Listen to your life. See it for the fathomless mystery that it is. In the boredom and pain of it no less than in the excitement and gladness; touch, taste, smell your way to the holy and hidden heart of it because in the last analysis all moment are key moments, and life itself is grace*".[5] As Parker Palmer says, "*Let your life speak*".[6]

I have divided the letter into these thirteen topics that I believe James wanted his friends to consider as challenging invitations to grow in faith. Each topic addresses common, daily issues that challenge our relationship to God; to our receiving and enjoying His loving presence. Mostly, each of these chapters is meant to be an invitation to a deeper intimacy with God. Each of the topics is an opportunity to pay attention to God in some personal areas of our daily life experiences. So, let's exegete these passages from the letter of James. Let's also let these texts exegete the experiences of our lives. And let's look for God's loving, intimate Word to us in it all.

---

[4] A.W. Tozer, *The Pursuit of God* (Harrisburg: Christian Publications, 1948), 61.
[5] Fredrick Buechner, *Now And Then: A Memoir of Vocation* (New York: Harpur Collins Publishers, 1991), 87.
[6] Parker Palmer, *Let Your Life Speak* (SanFrancisco: Jossey-Bass: A Wiley Co., 2000).

TESTING FAITH

A good teacher may start a course by inviting her class to do a pre-test to find out what her students don't know. This is not meant to punish them, but to find out what they still need to learn. At the beginning of a new a class, a teacher might say, *"Well, let's find out what you know."* Maybe on a piece of paper she'll have you write down everything you know about this or that topic. Then the teacher will gather all of the papers together and look through them and think, *"Hmmm, they know very little about this and that topic; so now I know what I need to teach them"*. The point of the test is not to fail students nor to punish them for not knowing enough about a subject, nor to pat the heads of the students who do well on that pre-test. Rather, the teacher wants to find out the students' areas for growth, in order to instruct them. Similarly, a musician will "test" his equipment before a performance. He will plug everything in and then say, *"Testing. Testing. One, two, three."* in to the microphone to see how it sounds. He doesn't punish the sound system if it's found lacking. He simply adjusts the volume, or treble, or bass to get it to where he wants it to make it sound right. Likewise, God "tests" us, not in order to shame us or punish us when we lack knowledge, or experience, or wisdom, or perseverance, but to find out where our vulnerable limitations are, so that He can lovingly comfort and strengthen us and heal us and deepen our experience of His love.

REFINING FAITH

Another analogy is how metal is tested to determine the purity or strength of its composition. Gold is refined in fire to separate it from and burn off any impure elements. Other metals may be intentionally strained by tensile force to the point of fracture to determine its character or strength. In the creation of a metal instrument, the item may be heated in a forge to a malleable point, and then intensely beaten, cooled, then heated again to improve its character. God may allow certain experiences in our lives to "test" the purity or strength of our faith. The dross may be exposed and burned off. The tensile strength may improve through strain and intensity. The apostle Paul was thinking of this analogy when he wrote, *"If anyone builds on this foundation using gold, silver, costly stones, wood, hay or straw, their work will be shown for what it is, because the Day will bring it to light. It will be revealed with fire, and the fire will test the quality of each person's work. If what has been built survives, the builder will receive a reward. If it is burned up, the builder will suffer loss but yet will be saved–even though only as one escaping through the flames"* (1 Cor. 3:12-15 NIV). Likewise, the writer of Hebrews wrote, *"Endure hardship as discipline; God is treating you as sons. For what son is not disciplined by his father? If you are not disciplined (and everyone undergoes discipline), then you are illegitimate children and not true sons. Moreover, we have all had human fathers who disciplined us and we respected them for it. How much more should we submit to the Father of our spirits and live! Our fathers disciplined us for a little while as they thought best; but God disciplines us for our good, that we may share in his holiness. No discipline seems pleasant at the time, but painful. Later on, however, it produces a harvest of righteousness and peace for those who have been trained by it."* (Heb. 12:7-11 NIV).

Each of James' "challenges" may expose certain limitations or impurities. Each may be seen as a "pre-test" to determine what we may need to learn more about, or they may be seen as opportunities to refine the character of our faith in the forge of God's discipline. One may argue over whether God creates the circumstances themselves. I am not going to address that question here. But one must at least say that God allows circumstances, and He can use the circumstances to help us persevere in becoming His stronger, finer disciples. Every experience in your life is an opportunity to strengthen the metal of your faith, to name specific issues that may be distracting you from God, to examine ways that you may grow closer to God. We are invited to ask God to *"test me LORD, and try me"* (Psalm 26:2 NIV).

REFLECT, EXAMEN AND EXERSISE

Following each chapter, I will invite you to reflect on some follow up questions and to engage in two Spiritual disciplines. The

11

questions are meant to engage one in personal reflection on each chapter's topic. The two Spiritual disciplines are meant to help you consider how each of these "challenges" might apply to your own journey towards wisdom and maturity. Ignatius Loyola developed a twice-daily discipline to help his 'Jesuit' order reflect on God's continuing leading in one's life. The "Examen" discipline invites one to prayerfully follow a five-step process of:

1. Quietly centering on the awareness of God's presence

2. Reviewing one's day with gratitude

3. Paying attention to one's emotions

4. Choosing one thing from the day to pray about

5. Looking forward to the next day with faith

Ignatius taught his community to speak with Jesus like a friend. I will ask you, as a friend, to use this same discipline to prayerfully reflect on each of the challenges found in James' letter with your friend, Jesus. He does not condemn us. And He meets us in these tough experiences and we can reflect on these challenges with gratitude for the past and hope for the future.

The second discipline found at the end of each chapter is an invitation to "exercise" some Spiritual muscles in trying some practical ways to apply what we learn from these challenges found in each chapter. These will not be exhaustive, and again, there is no condemnation for failing at them, or not even trying them. Rather, see if there may be some things to try that may help you grow in strengthening your faith in some of these life "tests". I hope you will receive these suggestions in the spirit of a fellow traveler who has some ideas that may help. Likewise, there are many books and other resources that may be of help to you on each of these topics.

Like any endeavor, a healthy, growing Christian life is developed through disciplined habits that help one move in the right direction, both in daily progress, and in regularly choosing the right, rather than the wrong direction in daily decisions. It can be compared to an athlete who trains for long stretches, in daily exercises for occasional bursts of athletic testing. In the 1996 Summer Olympics, sprinter Michael Johnson set world records in both the 200 and the 400-meter races. He was only able to accomplish this through training daily, over ten years, to progressively shave one second at a time off of his performances. In the introduction to his memoir 'Slaying the Dragon' he wrote, *"Success is found in much smaller portions than most people realize. A hundredth of a second here or sometimes a tenth there can determine the fastest man in the world. At times we live our lives on a paper-thin edge that barely separates greatness from mediocrity and success from failure. Life is often compared to a marathon, but I think it is more like being a sprinter: long stretches of hard work punctuated by brief moments in which we are given the opportunity to perform at our best".*[7]

---

[7] Michael Johnson, *Slaying the Dragon*, (New York: HarperCollins, 1996), xviii

Though there is no aspect of the Christian life that is a "performance" that includes "success" or "failure", a "great" spiritual life involves growth. And growth takes long stretches of simple, regular disciplined obedience with occasional bursts of crises when God allows opportunities to test and strengthen our faith. Evelyn Underhill wrote, *"If we ask of the saints how they achieved spiritual effectiveness, they are only able to reply that, insofar as they did it themselves, they did it by love and prayer. A love that is very humble and homely; a prayer that is full of adoration and of confidence. Love and prayer, on their lips, are not mere nice words; they are the names of tremendous powers, able to transform in a literal sense human personality and make it more and more that which it is meant to be—the agent of the Holy Spirit in the world. Plainly then, it is essential to give time or to get time somehow for self-training in this love and this prayer, in order to develop those powers. It is true that in their essence they are "given," but the gift is only fully made our own by a patient and generous effort of the soul. Spiritual achievement costs much, though never as much as it is worth. It means at the very least the painful development and persevering, steady exercise of a faculty that most of us have allowed to get slack".*[8]

I end each chapter with a prayer. This is an invitation for you to join me in surrendering all of these life and faith challenges to God. I

---

[8] Evelyn Underhill, *The House of The Soul and Concerning the Inner Life*, (Eugene: Wipf and Stock Publishers, 2004), 17.

trust that God is with us, and for us. He loves us unconditionally and never condemns us in the midst of these challenges, but invites us into these opportunities to grow in His loving work of producing His fruit of the character of Jesus in us and through us. I end each prayer with a question mark after the "Amen". The word "amen" simply means: "Let it be so". I am asking you if you agree, if you really want it "to be so in your life". It's a friendly question, and I hope you will respond to each of God's friendly invitations to grow in Him with a friendly invitation of your own, to say to God, "Yes, let it be so in my life".

WHO WAS JAMES?

I want to give you a little bit of contextual background to our study. The first "context" is who this James fellow was. I think it is important for us to get into the head of our author as best we can. I think I count four guys called "*James*" in the New Testament. Though some people have argued for (or assumed) this James to be one of the three other guys, I am assuming (with the scholars whom I believe to be the best) that our author is "*James, the Lord's brother*" (Mark 6:3). This is the assumption of Origen (c. A.D. 185–253), Eusebius (c. 265–340), and Jerome (c. 340–420).[9]

---

[9] Donald W. Burdick, James (Expositor's Bible Commentary, Vol. 12, Frank E. Gaebelein Ed., Grand Rapids: Zondervan, 1981), 161.

Jerome, writing early on in church history, and quoting Hegesippus' account of James from the fifth book of his lost Commentaries says: "*After the apostles* (besides the 12 original apostles and St. Paul) *James the brother of the Lord, surnamed the Just*" (that was one of his nicknames) *was made head of the Church of Jerusalem. This one was holy from his mother's womb. He drank neither wine nor strong drink, ate no flesh, never shaved or anointed himself with ointment or bathed. He alone had the privilege of entering the Holy of Holies, since indeed he did not use woolen vestments but linen and went alone into the temple and prayed in behalf of the people, insomuch that his knees were reputed to have acquired the hardness of camels' knees.*"[10] So James was the first senior pastor of all the churches that made up the Church of Jerusalem, which is the very first church.

These are some interesting facts about James. He drank no alcohol and was a vegetarian, so maybe a little dower, not a real party animal. He never shaved or anointed himself with ointment or bathed, so imagine a lot of hair and a bit smelly. He had the privilege of being the only one (maybe the only Christian) to enter the inner sanctum of the holiest center of the Temple. So, maybe, even though he was the lead pastor of the Christian Church in Jerusalem, he might have continued to operate as a Hebrew priest or at least have the exclusive privileges of the High Priest at times. And don't you love the description that (probably because he prayed

---

[10] Jerome, *Lives of Illustrious Men* (Princeton: Aeterna Press. 2016), 9.

so much) his knees had grown hard callouses like a camel's. Old "James the Just" was also nicknamed, "Old Camel Knees". James prayed so much for people, and not just for the Christian people, but for the Hebrew people as well, for all the people of Jerusalem, to come to know, love, and serve Jesus.

LIKE A FATHER TO THE CHURCH

1 Cor. 15:3-8 describes James as being one of the persons the risen Christ showed himself to. 1 Cor. 9:5 mentions James in a way that suggests James had been married. We also see James in Acts a few times. We find him in Acts 15. Remember, he is the one who makes the final decision for the Church. He's the senior pastor of the big Church. Paul and Barnabas had been out telling the good news to everybody in the whole Gentile world. But, as they were going along, behind them would come all these guys we call "Judaizers" who were telling the new Gentile followers of Jesus that they had to also follow all of the Hebrew cultural traditions of the Law. So Paul and Barnabas, and some of those Judaizers went back to Jerusalem to kind of argue their cases before the leaders of the Church. After hearing all the arguments, it is James who stands up and makes the decisive decision. I am so grateful that he did. It's one of the first greatest decisions of the church. James stands up and he makes this point that, no, the Gentiles are free in Christ. You

Jews who want to continue in those customs, that's fine, but we're not going to put that on the Gentiles. Wow. It was a huge decision.

In Acts 12, when Peter is miraculously busted out of prison by the angel, the angel says, *"Go tell James"*. It's this James, because he was seen as the leader of the Church. In Acts 21, Paul delivers money that he collects from all these Gentile churches, because the Jerusalem Church was in trouble. He brought it to Jerusalem and gave it to James to distribute. In Gal. 2, Paul lists James with Peter and John, as the three "pillars" of the Church, and who will minister to "the circumcised" (that is the Jews) in Jerusalem, while Paul and his fellows will minister to the Gentiles. So in a sense, James is like a father to the Church. He's one of those Spiritual fathers (or mothers) that I think God wants us all to become. And it's the point of God's work in our lives to help us to grow in that kind of wisdom and maturity.

There are two Greek Orthodox Hymns about James. One says:
> *As the Lord's disciple you received the Gospel,*
> *O righteous James;*
> *As a martyr you have unfailing courage;*
> *As God's brother, you have boldness;*
> *As a hierarch, you have the power to intercede.*
> *Pray to Christ God that our souls may be saved.*[11]

---

[11] Troparion (Tone 4).

The other says:

> *When God the Word, the Only-begotten of the Father,*
> *Came to live among us in these last days,*
> *He declared you, venerable James,*
> *to be the first shepherd and teacher of Jerusalem*
> *And a faithful steward of the spiritual Mysteries.*
> *Therefore, we all honor you, O Apostle.*[12]

Josephus & Hegesippus record James' death in Jer. in 62AD. The high priest Ananias assembled a council of judges who condemned James "on the charge of breaking the law," then threw him from the summit of the Temple in Jerusalem, then stoned him, and at last broke his skull with a fuller's club. Ananias really wanted to make sure he was dead! He silenced the man, but God's Word continues to speak through him 2,000 years later. There are two main theories about when James wrote his letter. Some scholars believe James wrote it near the end of his life, while others believe it was written as early as 50AD. If the earlier date is right, this may be the first New Testament document of the Church.[13]

EPISTLE OF STRAW?

---

[12] Kontakion (Tone 4)

[13] Jerome, *Lives of Illustrious Men* (Princeton: Aeterna Press, 2016), 9.

You may have heard that the letter of James has sometimes been called an *"epistle of straw"*. Have you ever heard that? The word "epistle" just means letter. And the fact is, this letter of James is not found in some of the earliest collections of Christian writing. Some people have argued that this is because it was rejected by some early Christians. Now, I would say that this had more to do with the fact that they just simply didn't have a copy of James. You can imagine what happened in the early Church. Churches would gather what they could get their hands on. And having any copies of anything was a problem because any form of any material to write on or with was very expensive. So, all people, and certainly especially Christian churches, had very little documents to work with. And so a lot of the early churches just didn't have copies of some parts of the New Testament. They had all the Old Testament, but until the third Century, some of the churches throughout the hinterlands simply didn't have copies of some of the smaller New Testament documents. The first Christian historian, Eusebius (c. 265-340) questioned the authority of James, not because of any of its contents, but simply because many Early Christian communities did not include it in their collections. But by the early third Century people like Eusebius and Jerome (c.340-420) unanimously agreed that the letter of James is in deed authoritative, New Testament Word of God. This was confirmed at the Council of Nicaea (325) and the Council of Carthage (397).

It was the great Reformer, Martin Luther (1483-1546) who most famously called the letter of James an "epistle of straw".[14] Now, he didn't mean that it is not meaningful. What he meant was James has very little of the basic gospel in it. Martin Luther was a great evangelist, and the letter of James itself is not a great evangelistic document. You can read the four gospels and get the basic good news of salvation in Christ. Rather, James is written to Hebrew people who are already Christians. And so it's not a document to try to help people understand what it means to become a Christian. It is rather a teaching for people who are already Christians, on how to live as Christians. And so sometimes people say, oh, you know, it's all about "works righteousness" or earning one's salvation through good work. And that would be the opposite of the message of Luther's favorite letter, Galatians! Well, I have to say, it isn't. James is based on understanding that we come to know Jesus through his gift of saving us. It's all grace. But once we are Christians, how do we live that way? How do we live the Christian life? How do we grow up in Jesus to become the spiritual mothers and fathers, wise and mature ones that Jesus wants us to be? That's what James is about.

STYLE OF WRITING

---

[14] Luther's Works, vol. 35, Word and Sacrament I (Philadelphia: Fortress, 1960), 362.

Though it is a first century letter from an old, Christian leader, James is written in a very old Hebrew kind of style. In fact, it is very similar in style to the Old Testament book of Proverbs. In Western style writing we tend to put things into a topical order, while Hebrew style is like throwing pebbles into a pond. An idea gets thrown out and we see how the ripples spread throughout the pond. But even before all the ripples are done, another pebble is tossed in. Sometimes the same topic is tossed out a few times in random order. It's like this idea, and watch how the ripples go out. Now this idea; ripples go out. That's kind of how James is. I have imposed my own idea of an order to the pebbles of the "challenge" topics. You'll see how many of the topics actually overlap and/or repeat some of the same ideas throughout the letter.

James also quotes Jesus gospel teaching throughout his letter. This is especially true of James' quoting from the Sermon on the Mount (Matt. 5-7). I will highlight those places where I notice James doing that. There are appendixes at the end of the book that will point this out. Appendix One shows where James quotes directly from the Sermon on the Mount, while appendix Two highlights where I have suggested in this book where James' thematic commentary on the whole of the Sermon on the Mount throughout his letter. I first heard Earl Palmer suggest that James is in fact primarily a commentary on the Sermon on the Mount.[15] Now, the Sermon on

---

[15] Earl Palmer, *The Book that James Wrote* (Eardmans Publishing Co. Grand Rapids, MI, 1997).

the Mount, it could be argued, was Jesus's exposition of the Hebrew Law. Appendix Three is my attempt to demonstrate that Jesus was indeed commenting on the Law. More than this, I would argue that Matthew was editing at least the first seven chapters of his gospel to be an obvious "New Exodus" story, as it too coincidentally parallels the Exodus story exactly. This makes sense, as we believe the story of Jesus to be the story of the new exodus of God's people from Spiritual slavery to eternal freedom.

There is also an authoritative tone to James' letter. He uses forty-six imperatives. That is a lot of commanding language. Imperatives are found in 60 of the 108 verses of James. In comparison, there are only 35 imperatives found in 1 Peter's 110 verses.[16] So, let's dig in! Let's listen to this old Father of our Church, as he authoritatively guides us in the way of knowing, loving, and serving Jesus Christ together.

Let's pray.

> *Lord, guide us in this study of your Spirit's Word through your brother, James. Help us to hear Your kind voice, Your loving words, Your our gentle invitations to grow in wisdom and maturity – for Your sake and Your glory – Amen?*

---

[16] Check out my book *"Listening to First Peter"*

REFLECT:

What kind of person do you think James was based on Acts 12, 15, 21, 1 Cor. 9, 15 & Gal. 2?

James was called "old camel knees". What might your Christian nickname be?

James has two Orthodox hymns written about him. What might a hymn about you contain?

EXAMEN:

In quiet attention to God's loving presence, reflect on the challenges of faith.

In gratitude, when have you been challenged by faith?

How are you feeling about faith?

What is something about faith that you can talk to God about?

What is something about faith you can look forward to?

Seek God's guidance, help, and understanding. Pray about faith.

EXERCISE:

Read all of the 'Sermon on the Mount' (Matthew 5-7) and the whole letter of 'James' is one sitting

Chapter 1

The Challenge of Trials

<u>James 1:1-8</u>

Hi! It's me, James, a servant of God and of the Lord
Jesus Christ. I'm writing this letter to you, the twelve
tribes scattered among the nations. Joy to you!
Consider it pure joy, my friends whenever you
encounter a multitude of trials of many colors.
Because you know that the testing of your faith
develops perseverance. Perseverance must continue
towards its end goal that we may be mature and
complete, lacking nothing. God doesn't want you to
lack anything. So if any of you is lacking wisdom, for
instance, you should ask God for it. And God, who
generously provides wisdom to everyone, without
finding fault, will give it to that person. The one who
is doubting this is like an ocean wave; blown around,
tossed by the wind. That kind of person isn't
expecting anything from God. Anyone who doesn't
trust God in the midst of these trials is double-
minded.

James starts his letter by announcing himself: *"Hi! It's me, James, I'm writing this letter to you."* (1:1). And he describes himself. He calls himself *"a servant of God and of the Lord Jesus Christ."* (1:1). He's a "servant". That's how he sees himself. We see that in the historical record about him. He was a servant, like a bishop, or senior pastor over the Church of Jerusalem. Originally, the Church of Jesus Christ was centered in Jerusalem, all of the first members were Jewish, and they met in small groups, as well as gathering at the Temple with other Jews. When Stephen was martyred (Acts 7) a great persecution drove all the Christians from Jerusalem into the surrounding countryside of Judea and Samaria (Acts 8:1). Only the apostles were left at the headquarters in Jerusalem. As the Church grew, it was made up of all kinds of little churches, meeting in all kinds of small gatherings, in communities all over the Roman world. James is writing to these people whom he sees as his parishioners, his church family members. They are the members of his church, though they were no longer in his city.

He calls them *"the twelve tribes scattered among the nations"* (1:1). He is identifying them (and all followers of Christ), as members of the continuing faith community of God's people, Israel. James' Church was basically made up of Jewish people who believed in Jesus. James saw them as the authentic continuation of that Old Testament faith; the ones who had accepted the promised Messiah, the Holy Scriptures, and who were continuing in the true teaching of God's Word. The Gentiles who joined the early Church were clearly aware that they were being grafted in to this Hebrew faith of "the twelve tribes", joining God's people as a part of Israel.

JOY TO YOU

James then salutes them with a greeting. He uses the Greek word "*chairein*", which literally means, "Joy to you!" He wishes them all "joy". This will be an important context for this whole letter. James is no sour old saint. He is a robust lover of God and people. He wishes all people to know the true joy of knowing, loving, and serving Jesus Christ, the living, reigning Lord. James knew Jesus well. He knew the power of God's love and joy that was the essence of being in relationship with our Lord. Too often people spoil the sweet, joyful Christian life with sour, stale religion. James wants no part of that for himself or for his beloved flock. May we all know the true joy of living in Christ that James knew!

Then James says a very interesting thing. He says, ***"Consider it pure joy, my friends*** (the word "*adelphoi*" here doesn't just mean male "brothers", but more broadly "family", "brothers and sisters", "friends") ***whenever you encounter a multitude of tests."*** (1:2). Here is our theme. Here's the first invitation to mature faith. It's the every day challenges that come our way. Living life will naturally present us with a series of experiences that will test the metal of our faith. And James encourages us to meet these challenges, with optimistic joy, seeing them as opportunities to see how strong our faith is, and where and how we might continue to grow towards wisdom and maturity.

This is a strange way to start a letter. There's no, *"Hey, how are you doing? How are things going down there in Samaria?"* There's nothing like that. He just jumps right in and starts talking about a uniquely Christian attitude and way of living. This has got to be important because this is what he starts with. **"Consider it pure joy, my friends whenever you encounter challenging tests."** (1:2). He is suggesting that we may regard any challenging trial as a joyful experience. And we might say, *"What!?"* You know, most of us, when encountering a trial will react by asking, *"What's going on here? Why is this happening? What did I do wrong to deserve this?"* Or – *"Why doesn't God like me right now that He's letting this happen?"* But James, writing to these people, whom he considers his beloved spiritual children, says, *"Look, friends, every trial you encounter, may be greeted with pure joy!"* He is quoting from Jesus' 'Sermon on the Mount' here. Jesus said, *"Blessed are you when people insult you, persecute you and falsely say all kinds of evil against you because of me. Rejoice and be glad, because great is your reward in heaven, for in the same way they persecuted the prophets who were before you"* (Matt. 5:11-12 NIV).

MULTI-COLORED TRIALS

In fact, James says something interesting about "trials". The adjective he uses literally means *"many colored"*. He calls them *"trials of many colors"* (1:2). There are all kinds of different colors of trials. Some are quite black. And some are grey. And some are yellow and blue and green. Our life challenges come in all kinds of colors. That may be a comforting way to think about life's trials. They are multi-colored experiences that I go through in life. They are normal. And as a follower of Jesus, I can count it pure joy to be in one of those. Why? He says, *"Because you know that the testing of your faith develops perseverance"* (1:3). That's the point of these trials. Our faith is not finished being developed. Our surrendered confidence in Jesus needs to be strengthened in many ways. The refining work of life's challenging, multi-colored trials are a way that our faith gets molded, and bent, and shaped into a stronger metal. That's what trials can do for us.

We may encounter trials more joyfully if we get to learn more about the things God wants us to understand through them. We get to grow in faith. We get to grow up in Christ. We get to become more and more those Spiritual mothers and fathers he wants us to be. The refining of our faith helps us in this. It does its work. Its work is to produce perseverance in you. Perseverance is the essence of faith over time. One might believe something right now. But, will you believe it over time? Faith needs perseverance, and perseverance needs faith. The word for perseverance is *"hypomonē"*. The 1st century philosopher Philo called *hypomonē* the queen of all virtues because perseverance makes all the other virtues last,[17] he said. *Hypomonē* is the stick-to-it-ness that we need to keep going. And we all need to grow in that kind of stick-to-it-ness. I would argue that today, more than ever, we are living in a time when there is very little stick-to-it-ness. Everything is disposable: stuff, habits, relationships, churches. We use people and things for a while and then toss them out when we've used them up, or when they no longer entertain us, or when they start to challenge us. That is the opposite of perseverance. And God, in His wisdom, wants to keep testing the metal of our faith, to keep refining us, so that we may become His more wise, mature, and loving followers.

THE END GOAL

James goes on to say that perseverance itself is in process of development in us. ***"Perseverance must continue towards its end goal"*** (1:4). These challenging trials in our lives have a final outcome. The goal is that we may be ***"mature and complete, lacking nothing"*** (1:4). It is all to build us up to make us mature and complete, not lacking anything, being completely whole. That's the purpose to everything we face in life. Everything is an opportunity for God to be building in us the kind of wholeness He

---

[17] Philo, *Delineation of the Mosaic Legislation for non-Jews* XLVI. (270) Loeb Classics.

longs for us. It is a growth in becoming more fully conformed to the character of Jesus. That's the trajectory we are meant to be on. We are being made more and more whole in the likeness of Jesus. And James knew that growing in that wisdom and maturity leads to that true, pure joy in Christ that he wished for all of us.

That word "complete" (*holokleros*) literally means to be whole, to be healthy, to be fixed. He's quoting Jesus who said, *"Be perfect (complete), therefore, as your heavenly Father is perfect (complete)"* (Matt. 5:48 NIV). This is not about moral perfection (an impossibility for imperfect human beings). God wants to make us whole, complete, lacking nothing of Spiritual vitality. We all have got a long way to go. The fact is we are all broken. We are not whole. Jesus wants to make us whole. Though we are saved in Him by grace, and we receive that free gift of grace by faith, just by saying thank you for all the work He has done to save us. But, once we have received that free gift of His saving work, there's a trajectory for our lives to grow in wisdom and maturity towards a goal. That goal is towards wholeness, healthiness, fixedness. This is what maturity is. It means to be whole, healthy, fixed.

When things get broken in my house, my family has a habit of putting the broken items on my dresser. I come home, and things have randomly appeared on my dresser. They are obviously broken. But there's no note. It's sort of this unspoken thing. Things break. I fix them. Now, I don't know if my family knows this, but I fix everything with *Shoe Goo*. I do. It's fantastic. It works on anything. But it doesn't last long if you put it in the dishwasher many times. The other night we were serving fish, and I pulled the fish platter out of the dishwasher, and it had melted the glue. Oops! I've got to re-*Shoe Goo* it. It's on my dresser right now. Sometimes the things that would show up on my dresser were things that are especially precious to my children when they were little. They would be sad about their shattered treasures being broken. But then they would bring it to my dresser, like offering a sacred thing on an altar - the magic dresser! Then I'd come home and I'd get the *Shoe Goo* and put it back together. Then I'd present it to them. It's whole! It's renewed!

That's the word picture here. Jesus wants to put us back together. We are all God's broken and shattered treasures. And he's desperate to put us back together. He wants us to grow in that wholeness, to be fixed, to grow in wisdom and maturity and the trajectory of being more like Jesus. Each of us, in our own unique way, are being shaped into the likeness of Jesus, to reflect His nature through our unique way. That's his whole point. God wants us to be not lacking anything we need. So God is using the trials of our lives to test our faith that we might be strengthened and give us perseverance, to grow us in wisdom and maturity. That's His end goal. And that's the goal, or the purpose of whatever you are facing right now, whatever is coming this week. It is a test of how strong your perseverance is, and how wise and mature you are. Now, you'll notice James is not saying God will give you whatever you *want*. Wisdom is the very skill to live life in a godly way. If you lack wisdom, ask for it. It starts with wanting it, expecting it, and asking God for it, then going through the challenging trials to get it and grow in it.

In his Genesee Diary, Henri Nouwen wrote, *"In Abraham Heschel's A Passion for Truth I read today the words of the Kotzker (Rabbi Menahem Mendl of Kotzk): "He who thinks that he has finished is finished." How true. Those who think that they have arrived, have lost their way. Those who think they have reached their goal, have missed it. Those who think they are saints, are demons. An important part of the spiritual life is to keep longing, waiting, hoping, expecting. In the long run, some voluntary penance becomes necessary to help us remember that we are not yet fulfilled. A good criticism, a frustrating day, an empty stomach, or tired eyes might help to reawaken our expectation and deepen our prayer: Come, Lord Jesus, come"*.[18]

All of us want our children to grow up to be wise and mature, to be independent and self-reliant adults. But, let's admit it, we don't want our kids to have to go through the very experiences that they need to go through that will develop wisdom and maturity, independence and self-reliance. We tend to want to protect them

---

[18] Henri Nouwen, *The Genesee Diary: Report from a Trappist Monastery*, (London: Darton, Longman and Todd Ltd., 1999), 133.

from the very experiences that they need to go through to get there. God loves us too much to keep us from trials that test the metal of our faith. These challenges deepen our wisdom and maturity. We don't have to believe that God causes a certain trial. But, we can trust that God is with us in every trial. He never abandons us (Heb. 13:5). He can even use these trials as invitations to experience His love in new ways; to deepen our relationship to Him and develop our maturity and wisdom - to make us whole.

TRUST FOR WHAT'S LACKING

James says, ***"God doesn't want you to lack anything. So if any of you is lacking wisdom, for instance, you should ask God for it. And God, who generously provides wisdom to everyone, without finding fault, will give it to that person"*** (1:5). God wants us to be whole. He wants us to be lacking nothing we need. So if you lack wisdom, ask God for it. Now, wisdom is not an intellectual answer to some question. Remember, this is a Hebrew letter from a Hebrew Christian. Every Hebrew knows that the beginning of wisdom is *"the fear of the Lord"* (Psalm 111:10). Is anybody lacking that fear of the Lord, that real understanding and right relationship with God, that maturity in putting faith into everyday life practice? Just ask God to give it. God is so generous with His wisdom. He doesn't reproach anyone for asking for it. He will generously give it.

I admit that sometimes I have trouble believing in God's generosity, or His lack of condemnation. I admit that sometimes I think God is not generous, that He gets mad at me for trivial things, or that He's not willing to give me what we need. Do we really believe that God is generous? Do we really believe that the God of the universe wants to give us the wisdom and maturity we need? Can we believe that? Do you really believe that God doesn't reproach us for asking for it? Do you really believe that God is able to give us wisdom and maturity? If you don't believe that, then I'd say you may be believing in a different god other than the one that is revealed in the Holy Scriptures. James says, when we ask for wisdom, we must believe and not doubt, because *"the one who is doubting (present tense) is like an ocean wave; blown around, tossed by the wind"* (1:6). I think James primarily means that this kind of "doubting" is distrusting the very character of God. Believing that God isn't generous, that he doesn't want to give you wisdom and maturity makes one a rudderless boat in the sea. You are out of sorts in a roiling ocean of doubt.

THE RUDDER OF FAITH

Liz and I went ocean kayaking recently. We borrowed some friends' kayaks, and we put them right in the water at the shore and floated out into the bay. Liz had used these kayaks before, so she was explaining them to me. She said, *"You see that little lever behind you. Pull that and your rudder will pop down. Then there's these little foot pedals that control the rudder. You have to adjust those with another little lever that's inside the kayak."* Now, I'm a big guy, and this was a little kayak. Liz is a lot smaller than me, and she was bending backwards and forwards in her kayak, adjusting levers and pedals all over the place. I could not even turn at all in my kayak. I was so pinched in that little hole. So I didn't bother. My rudder never came down, and my feet never found the pedals. I didn't say anything because I didn't want to ruin our little outing. What's Liz going to say to me, *"Well, don't be so fat"?* I thought, *"Forget it, I'm just going to sit here and paddle".* But I kept thinking, *"If I really got hit by any kind of big wave out here, or if there was any kind of real wind, I would not be able to control this thing. I would be tossed all over the place. I can't steer. I can't glide. I'm at the mercy of these waves that could capsize me any minute!"* We did have a lovely time, but only because the water was so calm and there was no wind. But life isn't always like that, is it? Life isn't always calm. When we hit those patches where the wind is up and where the storm is on us, if we have no rudder, we are blown around. We can be blown right out of the water, can't we? Some of you have been there, and that's what happened. The rudder we need is perseverant belief and trust in the right God. It's belief in the very character of God; that he is generously providing for you, guiding you through life's trials, without reproach, towards wisdom and maturity.

The wind and waves of life's challenges are going to buffet us. Without the rudder of perseverant faith we will be tossed about, or even drowned. James says, *"That kind of person isn't expecting anything from God. Anyone who doesn't trust God in the midst of these trials is double-minded"* (1:7, 8). The word for "double-minded" James uses there is *"dipsychos"*. It means to be split in one's loyalties. The one who is doubting the work of God in using the trials of life, and not participating in it, not intimately meeting with God in it, and not learning perseverance from it, may be split in two directions; trusting God half way, but trying to trust their own control over these situations at the same time. We really can't do both. True faith is recognizing that my whole life is in God's loving hands, and that I can really control nothing. Let's be single-minded in trusting God in the trails we face. Let's have our minds and hearts focused on the trustworthy God who has us in His loving hands, and see that He is preparing us to be the spiritual mothers and fathers we get to be for our communities.

James says we need to be single-minded in believing that God is going to take us to that end goal of wholeness in our lives, that we need to trust that God is generously moving us in that direction. God uses the trials of our lives to get us there, to build us in that direction, and to give us the very perseverance we need. He is not saying it's going to be pleasant, but He is saying it's what we need.

Let's pray.

God, thank you for your word. Thank you for revealing who you are, the true God that we want to get to know so that we can trust you in the midst of trials. And, God, I know that right now there are people who are facing unimaginable trials, trials that make us feel like we are drowning. God, we pray that you would give people that rudder of trust, and that we may be surrounded by your people and your encouragement, that we would turn to you to trust you in the face of trials. We are going to find ourselves in many multi-colored trials. God, help us to remember who you are and that these are opportunities for us to grow in what you want to teach us, to grow in wholeness, creating that character of Jesus in us more and more. Lord, help us to turn our lives to you in the midst of trials. Amen?

REFLECT:

How can a trial be a joyful experience?

How might God be using a trial to test your faith right now?

How are you being asked to persevere?

When have you felt like quitting?

Do you really believe God is generous?

Do you really believe God doesn't reproach our asking?

Do you really believe God is able to give you wisdom?

EXAMEN:

In quiet attention to God's loving presence, reflect on the challenges of trials.

In gratitude, when have you been strengthened by facing trials?

How are you feeling about trials?

What is something about trials that you can talk to God about?

What is something about facing trials you can look forward to?

Seek God's guidance, help, and understanding. Pray about facing trials.

EXERCISE:

Make a list of the trials God is allowing in your life.

Talk to God about how you feel about each one.

Consider how each one is testing the metal of your faith.

Consider what God may be inviting you into through these trials.

Chapter 2

The Challenge of Privileges

James 1:9-12

Christian believers who are in modest circumstances should consider their privileges. Wealthy Christians should consider their humility. Circumstances are going to disappear like wild flowers. The sun comes up with scorching heat and withers them, and their blossoms fall and their beauty decays. Just like withering flowers, any possessions will disappear, even while they're being accumulated. When you persevere under life's challenges you are blessed, because when one has passed through a challenge, one will receive the ultimate reward of life which God has promised to those who love Him.

PRIVILEGED CIRCUMSTANCES

The next inviting opportunity to grow in faith that James turns to is the whole topic of privilege. One of the greatest areas of challenge in our spiritual lives comes through how we handle the life circumstances we are born into. Life's privileges are disproportionately distributed amongst us. We all experience many unfair advantages and disadvantages. We are born into certain circumstances; accidents of gender, wealth, skin color, genetic type, education, parents, friends, neighborhood, century. We cannot take credit for any of these things. We were not smart enough to pick our genes or our geography. This is simply where and when we find ourselves. The online article *'Talking to Students About Privilege and Power'* states, *"People often talk about how "lucky" they are to enjoy certain benefits and opportunities in their lives. Expressing gratitude is great, but sometimes saying "luck" instead of "privilege" means we miss an opportunity to think critically about power and the structures that create and maintain an unequal society. Privilege is any unearned benefit, opportunity or advantage given to people because of their identity. When we talk about privilege, we're asking people to think critically about power and the way that it can sometimes be held by certain people because of one or more facets of their identify – things like race, religion, gender, sexuality, class/wealth or ability. It is important from the outset to recognize that privilege itself is not a bad thing, so young people should not be made to feel ashamed if they recognize that*

41

they are privileged. It is useful instead to see it as a reminder.
Recognizing privilege is an opportunity to foster empathy, increase
understanding and play our own part in correcting some of the
inequities that exist in our society".[19]

We all have privileges. There's always someone else's life we can
compare our own to, and see that we have some advantages they
don't. At any point in history, in any community, there is someone
with less privilege than our own. Right now, there is someone that
envies your privileges. Meanwhile, there is always someone we can
compare ourselves to who has advantages over us. There are
individuals and groups of people whom you can think of right now
whose privileges you envy. I think it was Theodore Roosevelt who
said, *"Comparison is the thief of Joy"*. That is so true. Let's just
admit it: we all get jealous of other people's privileges. We all
believe that if we just had certain advantages that those "winners"
possess (more money, better looks, that guy's lucky break) we would
be kinder, more generous, and happier people. We envy those
"winners". We might especially think that if we had the advantage
of wealth, most of our problems would be over. But, I remember
reading about a study of ten people who had won significant
amounts of money through lotteries. Nine of the winners said later
that they wished it had never happened, that their lives were worse
off than before they had their sudden luck. The only one who did

---

[19] The Line, "Talking to students about privilege and power," The Line, n.d.,
https://www.theline.org.au/talking-to-students-about-privilege-and-power

not regret his sudden fortune had changed nothing in his life except buying a new truck. As with any other challenge in our lives, it is not about the thing itself, but about how we respond to it. That's the challenge. One day, when my son was about ten, he asked me for my Visa number. When I asked him what he wanted it for, he said he wanted to buy something on the Internet. I was a little concerned, so I asked him to show me what he was engaged with on our computer. He showed me this site that he had looked up where he could give money to people in need. He handed me $100 in cash (all his savings) and asked me to let him use my Visa to give to those who had less than him. I said to him, *"But son, that's all your money. Are sure you want to give it ALL away?"* He said, *"Dad, I have everything I need. These people have nothing"*. I gave him my Visa!

James says, ***"The Christian believers who are in modest circumstances should consider their privileges. The wealthy Christians should consider their humility"****(1:9, 10a)*. James is talking to, and talking about Christians. He uses the term *"ho alelphos"* (the brother). He means Christian people. This is for us. He is contrasting people of modest means with those who are rich. So we're dealing here with our economic privileges, and what differences a Christ-centered life will have in whatever economic situation we find ourselves in. The psalmist wrote, *"How priceless is your unfailing love! Both high and low among men find refuge in the shadow of your wings. They feast on the abundance of your* *house; you give them drink from your river of delights. For with you is the fountain of life; in your light we see light"* (Ps. 36:7-9). Those in both high and low positions can thank God for His unfailing love and all the natural goodness, beauty and truth all around us in the very fountain of life.

My wife, Liz started a journal of things she is thankful for. She was inspired by Ann Voskamp's book, *'One Thousand Gifts'*.[20] Liz is aiming to write a thousand things down in the little book she's using. I think she might even mention me a few times. Some of the things she has written down are even the "multi-colored" trials that have come our way. Some of these we can already see as helpful for growing in faith and perseverance. Sometimes she has written down things that we are grateful for in the midst of trials. Even while experiencing trials there are many great blessings all around us. Most of the things she is writing down are the many pleasures we are so privileged to experience. Practicing gratitude is a great discipline to help one be alert to life's joys especially in the midst of trials.

HIGH AND LOW POSITIONS

This is some tough stuff that James is saying to us. He says we need to pay attention to our "low position" (NIV). The word James uses here means our "downgradedness". It's a sense of appreciating the

---

[20] Ann Voskamp, *One Thousand Gifts: A Dare to Live Fully Right Where You Are,* (Grand Rapids: Zondervan, 2010).

ultimate end of our lives and what the ultimate purpose of our lives is. The ultimate end of our earthly lives is our ultimate fragility, the fact that none of this is going to last. Even if you have the experience of the greatest of privileges, your life is but a tiny blip in history. It's very fragile and it's very limited. Everything is going to turn to dust, including our own bodies. The ultimate goal of our spiritual lives is not to attain, or maintain the privileges of personal power and prestige. It is to hold these privileges humbly, and to use them for the good of others. It is to surrender all of our personal resources to the mission of the Kingdom of God, which includes actively working for justice and mercy (Micah 6:8). Having or not having privilege is not really the issue. It's one's attitude about one's personal circumstances and how one engages in the opportunities one has to serve the Kingdom of God. What one does with the privileges that one possesses is vital. One can either squander them on selfish pursuits, or spend them in the pursuit of justice and mercy. So James is offering a right perspective on what we should pay attention to, what we should focus our minds on, what we should concentrate on, what we should think about. This is a test of what our faith is ultimately in.

Remember what the apostle Paul said to his friends in Philippi. He said, *"I have learned to be content whatever the circumstances. I know what it is to be in need, and I know what it is to have plenty"* (Phil. 4:11b, 12a NIV). Paul experienced times of having positions of powerful, personal influence. He experienced other times of oppressive, systemic abuse, but he was able to say, *"I have learned the secret of being content in any and every situation, whether well fed or hungry, whether living in plenty or in want"* (4:12b NIV). The secret is, that it's not about the circumstances. It's about our attitude in those circumstances. It's about how we are living in whatever circumstances we are in. James doesn't say one of these is better than the other. He is saying that whatever situation you find yourself in, one's attitude in the circumstances is a test of one's true faith. We don't have do be content with our circumstances, but we can be content in our circumstances.

My friend, Christopher Page uses the word "equanimity" for this state of being content in, though not necessarily with one's circumstances. He concedes that it is difficult to point to a single text or book where this concept is dealt with originally, or extensively. But he believes it is a concept found throughout the stories of the Christian desert mystics. In the ancient mystic literature, the word most often used for this concept may be *apatheia*. The main text where that word is found is the five volumes of *The Philokalia*, where it is most often translated as "dispassion". This may sound to modern ears as close to the Buddhist concept of "detachment", but the Desert Fathers were not detached from personal emotions, merely isolated from worldly engagements. The contemporary word "equanimity" captures the essence of Christian contentment without some of the negative baggage of "dispassion" or "detachment". John Eudes Bamberger defines it as "a relatively permanent state of deep calm, arising from the full and harmonious integration of the emotional life, under the influence of love."[21]   According to the Orthodox Bishop Kallistos Ware, *"The concept connotes not repression but reorientation, not inhibition but freedom; having overcome the passions, we are free to be out true selves, free to love others, free to love God. Dispassion, then, is no mere mortification of the passions but their replacement by a new and better energy."*[22] From The Philokalia:

> *"Accept with equanimity the intermingling of good and evil, and then God will resolve all inequity."*[23]

> *"The offspring of equanimity is love."*[24]

> *"Equanimity is established through remembrance of God."*[25]

> *"This, surely, is the sign of equanimity: to remain calm and fearless in all things because one has received by God's grace the strength to do*

---

[21] John Eudes Bamberger "Introduction" *Evagrius Ponticus The Praktikos & Chapters on Prayer,* lxxxiv
[22] Introduction to *The Ladder of Divine Ascent,* 32.

[23] St. Mark the Ascetic vol. 1
[24] St. Theodore The Great Ascetic vol. 2
[25] Ilian The Presbyter vol. 3

anything"[26]

"The promised land is dispassion, from which
spiritual joy flows like milk and honey."[27]

Those in humble circumstances can set their hearts on the fact that
their struggle is an invitation to meet God in deep faith, an
opportunity to grow in wisdom and maturity. Those in privileged
circumstances can set their hearts on the fact that their privilege is a
test; an opportunity to grow in wisdom and maturity through helping
others. Those in humble circumstances can set their hearts on
gratitude for what they do have, especially their riches in Christ.
Those in privileged circumstances can recognize that life is not about
personal satisfaction, but humble service, humble engagement in
God's justice and mercy. Those in humble circumstances can be
grateful that they are free from the burdens of the responsibilities of
privilege. We might say, *"Well, I wouldn't mind a little bit of that*
burden". But, those in positions of power and privilege are
accountable for the awesome responsibility given to them by God.
They must use their power and privilege for His purposes. That is a
huge responsibility, and a serious burden. Remember that Jesus
said, *"From everyone who has been given much, much will be*
demanded; and from the one who has been entrusted with much,
much more will be asked" (Luke 12:48b). Those in humble

---

[26] St. Peter of Damaskos vol. 3
[27] St. Gregory of Sinai vol. 4

48

circumstances can set their hearts on what is of eternal value while those in privileged circumstances can set their hearts on what is of eternal value. Really, it's the same challenge. This is not really about how much privilege one has. It's about our attitude towards it. Our privileges are simply vehicles to test the metal of our faith.

IT'S ALL GOING TO DISSAPPEAR

Besides, James says, *"Circumstances are going to disappear like wild flowers. The sun comes up with scorching heat and withers them, and their blossoms fall and their beauty dies"* (1:10b, 11a). James is quoting from Isaiah 40. Likewise, the apostle Peter quoted the exact same thing about the fragility of life, and the fleetingness of our circumstances writing, *"All people are like grass. All their glory, like, everything you could look at, it's like the flowers in the field. The grass withers, the flowers fall because of the breath of the Lord that blows on them, and surely the people are like grass. Grass withers, the flowers fall. But the word of our God stands forever"* (1 Peter 1:24, 25). Pretty quickly, like summer flowers, our lives, our resources, our privileges will disappear. In the twinkling of an eye, it's gone. I know some of you didn't have to wait for death for it to disappear. We are living in a time when people have seen their personal prestige and security disappear overnight. James says, *"Just like disappearing flowers, any possessions will disappear, even while they're being accumulated"* (1:11b). The Psalmist wrote, *"Surely the lowborn are but a breath, the highborn are but a lie. If weighed on a balance, they are nothing; together they are only a breath"* (Psalm 62:9 NIV).

Then James says, ***"When you persevere*** (and here's that word *"hypomonē"* again) ***under the test** (of privilege) **you are blessed, because when one has passed the test** (of privilege) **one will receive the ultimate summit of life which God has promised to those who love Him"*** (1:12). Privilege is a test. And those who stay true to the right attitude and responsibility in their circumstances have achieved the height of maturity in Christ. They have the blessed wisdom of Christ-likeness that is better than any of the privileges, possessions, or pleasures of this world. It is worth any suffering and sacrifice in this life to gain that. Again, James is quoting right from Jesus's Sermon on the Mount and saying that true blessings are not the privileges of prestige and pleasure. Truly blessed are *"the poor in spirit"*, *"those who mourn"*, *"the meek"*, *"those who hunger and thirst for righteousness"*, *"the merciful"*, *"the pure in heart"*, *"the peacemakers"*, *"those who are persecuted because of righteousness"*. Again, in his Sermon on the Mount, Jesus is quoting straight from the Old Testament. Here's Psalm 84: *"Lord Almighty, blessed is the one who trusts in you"*. See, it's not those who have a lot of privilege in this life who are truly blessed. But that's the North American dream, isn't it? We are driven to excel in acquiring and hoarding any kind of privilege over others. It's twisted, and it's the opposite of what God would want for us. He wants to build us into wise and mature spiritual people. That's what it means to be blessed; trusting in God. Here's one of my favorite passages in the Old Testament: *"This is what the Lord says: 'Cursed is the one who trusts in humanity, in human beings, who depends on flesh for strength, whose heart turns away from the Lord. That kind of person is like a bush in the wasteland. They will not even see prosperity when it comes'"* (Jer. 17:5, 6 NIV). The incessant drive for greater human privilege is Spiritually bankrupt. It leaves one arid and sad like a dry bush in a desert wasteland, not even appreciating the riches one already has.

Isn't that the kind of world we live in, where it doesn't really matter how much people have? They are in despair because they never have enough. Apparently, when he was the richest man on earth, J. Paul Getty was asked how much money was enough. He famously replied, *"Just a little bit more"*. When you look to worldly privileges to give you meaning in life, to meet your significance, to meet your purpose, it'll always come up short. You feel like a bush in the wasteland, dwelling in the parched places of the desert, in a salt land where no one really lives. Again, I think that describes the pursuit of pleasure and prestige that is all around us. But, *"blessed is the one who trusts in the Lord, whose confidence is in Him"* (Jer. 17:7 NIV). To be blessed means to be persevering in trusting God through the trials and temptations of this life. Some of the toughest trials and temptations come with the circumstances of our lives, the privileges we have that we either hoard for ourselves, or spend in loving service to God. Sometimes we test God with our complaints about

Him not giving us want we wish we had, or allowing trials we wish we didn't have. God may be challenging us with how we invest every privileged circumstance we do have.

Let's pray.

God, we thank you for your word. We thank you even when you say some tough things. And, God, I am standing under the conviction of your word to ask myself these questions. We all have privileges that we have been given. Help us to use everything in our lives to serve You. Help us to not compare ourselves to anyone else. God, give us a right perspective and response to the circumstances of our lives, whatever they might be, that we would turn to you in faith and trust and act like it. Amen?

REFLECT:

What privileges do you possess?

What resources has God uniquely given you that could help others with?

What advantages do you wish you had?

What invitation is God extending to you through your privileges?

What might God be saying to you through what you have or don't have?

When have comparisons stolen your joy?

EXAMEN:

In quiet attention to God's loving presence, reflect on the challenges of privilege.

In gratitude, when have you been strengthened by humility and gratitude?

How are you feeling about your privileges?

What is something about your privileges that you can talk to God about?

What is something about your privileges you can look forward to?

Seek God's guidance, help, and understanding. Pray for humility and gratitude

EXERCISE:

Start a gratitude journal

Chapter 3

The Challenge of Temptations

<u>James 1:13-18</u>

When one experiences temptation, one should not say, "God is tempting me". Because God is never tempted by evil, nor does God tempt anyone to do evil. One is tempted when one is captivated and seduced by a selfish desire. As one actively engages with that desire, a seed is conceived in one's life. That seed grows and is eventually born as a distraction from God. And, when that distraction grows up, it becomes death. Don't be deceived, friends. Every good and helpful thing we experience is a beam of light from God, the originator of all light, who never changes or hides in shadows. God chose to bring us to birth through His Word. We get to be the first fruits of all that God has created.

WHERE TEMPTATIONS COME FROM

James tells his friends, *"When one experiences temptation, one should not say, "God is tempting me. Because God is never tempted by evil, nor does God tempt anyone to do evil"* (1:13). God is never tempting us into doing anything wrong, but He certainly allows the temptations we naturally face in this life to refine us and build us up in perseverant trust in Him. We may not like it, but the daily temptations we face are the very kinds of opportunities that God allows and even utilizes to strengthen us in a more robust faith.

Now, God is not the one doing the tempting. Temptations show up daily like seductive sirens on rocky shores calling out to troubled sailors. James describes the process of falling for these seductive temptations using the metaphor of sex: *"One is tempted when one is captivated and seduced by a selfish desire. As one actively engages with that desire, a seed is conceived in one's life. That seed grows and is eventually born as a distraction from God. And, when that distraction grows up, it becomes death"* (1:14, 15).

God didn't send that temptation. My own natural selfishness is always at work. My self-serving desires are in constant want of being satiated. They regularly seduce me into believing that I can be satisfied through things rather than God. As we entertain our desires with selfish actions, our lives are impregnated with the seeds of those actions (guilt, regret, shame, frustration). These seeds grow in us and flourish to become what the bible calls "sin". Sin is not the actions, but the condition of being distracted from God. Sin is the steering wheel of one's life being turned away from God and driving in a direction away from God. As that trajectory is followed, it continues on its way towards fragmenting our lives. We become cut off from healthy connections to God, self, and others. This is the state we live in. All around us is the fragmentation of all of existence. God's original intention for wholeness is replaced with a shattered world of broken relationships. We are fragmented and conflicted in our relationships with God, each other, creation, and our selves. The inevitable result is the deadness of one's relationship with God and of one's Spiritual life. St. Paul described this when he wrote, "*The wages of sin is death*" (Rom. 6:23). He meant the natural result of pursuing a distracting course away from God is the death of our Spiritual connection to God.

Temptations themselves are not "sin". Jesus was tempted, but he never "sinned" (Heb. 4:15). As a human being, Jesus regularly encountered the exact same kinds of seductive forces that distract all people from God. But he was never distracted. He remained in perfect relationship with the Father and the Spirit. Jesus was "*led by the Spirit up into the wilderness to be tempted by the Devil*" (Matt. 4:1). Jesus was in the very center of God's will in the middle of His temptations. The trial of those temptations was a direct invitation of the Holy Spirit for Jesus to face these challenges as an opportunity to practice His centeredness in God. God allows the same tempting challenges into our lives as invitations to center our hearts in God.

In his wilderness encounter with Satan the Tempter (Matt. 4:1-11), Jesus faced three archetypal distractions from relationship with God: pleasure (satisfying hunger by turning stones into bread), passivity (just falling off the peak of the Temple and letting God serve you), and power (taking dominion over all the kingdoms of the world). These are fundamentally the basic kinds of *"cravings of the flesh, lust of the eyes, and the pride of life"* (1 Jn. 2:16 NIV) that we face every day. Jesus refuted each temptation by rebuking the Devil's twisting of the Scriptures with his own bible quotes, by denying the allure of these distracting false promises, and by dismissing Satan outright. He passed the test!

TEMPTATIONS ARE NOT THE PROBLEM

Temptations are not the problem. Nor is our natural propensity to desire things the problem. We have natural desires for things like food, sex, comfort, and community. And God has given us natural means of satisfying these desires in healthy ways. The problems come when we indulge these desires in unhealthy ways; when we give them the obsessive attentions they do not deserve. That's when it "conceives" sin. This is part of the challenge. Will we focus too much on unhealthy obsessions with any natural desires, or will we put them in their place under our first desire – our loving relationship

57

with God. Jesus didn't concentrate on the tempting distractions. He concentrated on God's Word. Later in his letter James will say, *"Surrender yourselves to God. But defy the Devil, and the devil will flee from you"* (4:7). So, the challenge is to not concentrate on the tempting distraction. Sometimes the most distracting thing is to be trying so hard to not do that bad thing. Instead, God invites us to be like Jesus and concentrate on God's Word; God's instructions, encouragements, and promises found in the bible. Sometimes, working hard at resisting sin we are actually entertaining that temptation so much it takes over our lives. We are actually letting it be conceived in our hearts and mind through the attention we give it. Jesus simply refuted, denied, and dismissed Satan with his biblically centered imagination. And when we do get momentarily distracted, by some temptation, we can likewise confess it, and then rebuke it, deny it, and dismiss it.

James says: *"Don't be deceived, friends!"* (1:16). He loves these people, and he doesn't want them to be tricked by Satan. Here is the word of God, the Holy Spirit speaking through James to us today. I hear God speaking to me through James with the same love, saying, *"My dear friend, don't be deceived by these seductive temptations. Don't be ignorant of how this all works. Don't be uninformed. Don't be fooled by Satan. Don't be blinded by the world. Don't be self-deluded, or willfully ignorant. Don't fail this test!"*

Hannah Whitall Smith wrote, *"Christian life is to be throughout a warfare; and that especially when seated in heavenly places in Christ Jesus, we are to wrestle against spiritual enemies there, whose power and skill to tempt us must doubtless be far superior to any we have ever heretofore encountered. As a fact, temptations generally increase in strength tenfold after we have entered into the interior life, rather than decrease. And no amount or sort of them must ever for a moment lead us to suppose we have not really found the true abiding place. Strong temptations are generally a sign of great grace, rather than of little grace ... And the very power of your temptations, dear Christian, therefore, may perhaps be one of the strongest proofs that you really are in the land you have been seeking to enter, because they are temptations peculiar to that land. You must never allow them to cause you to question the fact of your having entered it."*[28]

A BEAM OF LIGHT

And, James has some more good news for us. We are not asked to just simply ignore the testing temptations. God has given us resources to meet these challenges. He has given us ways and means to come through each test with greater strength and growth. James reminds us that, **"every good and helpful thing we experience is a beam of light from God, the originator of all light, who never**

---

[28] Hannah Whitall Smith, *The Christian's Secret of a Happy Life*, (New Jersey: Spire Books, Fleming H. Revell Co., 1942), 84, 85.

changes or hides in shadows" (1:17). James is quoting the Sermon on the Mount here: "*...how much more will your Father in heaven give good gifts to those who ask him!"* (Matt. 7:11 NIV). See, all good things are from God. We can thank God for all the good things we experience every day. There are good things in every life, every day. We can trust that God won't change. He won't suddenly try to trick us. He is plainly revealing light through His own good nature through the goodness, truth, and beauty we see all around us. Like beams of light from heaven, God is shining a flashlight beam of His goodness throughout your world, showing you His good presence.

But, not everything comes from God. Temptations come out of the shadows, straight from our enemy, Satan (the Tempter). And God will use the dark temptations we face, the things Satan and the world are throwing at us all the time, which God even allows, as a refining test of our faith. So be alert. Be watching for those beams of the light of goodness. Thank God for them. And be watching for those temptations. Avoid them. Don't be distracted by temptations. Turn any goodness into thankfulness to God. Turn any temptation into confession, rebuke, denial, and dismissal.

A WAY THROUGH

Here's another thought: Not all good things are pleasant, or pleasurable. God provides what we need, not necessarily what we want. Sometimes, the very things we need to develop the kind of

60

strong metal of faith we need, comes through the experiences of meeting and beating life's temptations. The denial of some pleasures, powers, and passivities develops the very strengths of character we need to be the kinds of Spiritual elders God is developing us into. Sometimes the temptations themselves may be a nagging noise alerting us to some area of growth that is needed in our lives. One time our family was traveling from a vacation at a remote cabin to a visit with friends in a big city. As we left the remote cabin, our van was rattling terribly. I thought, *These roads are awful!*" But, as we got off the remote, country roads, and on to the smooth highway, our van was still making terrible noises. So, being the great, handyman dad that I am, I told my son to jam a hockey stick against the side door to stop it from rattling. Along the way, the van kept rattling, so I kept turning the stereo up. Finally, as we were flying along the highway, my wife, Liz was intently looking at the passenger's side mirror. She suddenly screamed, *Stop the car!!*" I pulled over to the side of the road and she jumped out and ran to the back of the van. When I joined her there she was staring at our back tire, crying. At first I thought we had run over a chicken and wondered why she was so sad about that. There were, what looked like feathers sticking out of our tire. Then I realized that these were the layers of metal and rubber materials that were ripped and splayed out off the tire. The only thing left between my most cherished loved ones and a disastrous blow out was a thin layer of inner tire rubber. Instead of listening to the warning sounds trying to get my attention about trouble in my life, I just kept tuning them out with a hockey stick against the door and louder music. How often do we ignore the warning signals in our lives? Sometimes, even the temptations in our lives are warning signals that something is in need of attention. Maybe your spiritual life is hanging by a thin layer of rubber between you and a major blow out. Pay attention to the warnings that temptations can be. They are invitations to draw closer to God, to draw more deeply from the endless wellspring of His love, to draw on more of the resources of God's goodness, truth, and beauty.

God will not let us experience a temptation beyond that, which is common human experience, nor beyond what we can endure, nor without providing a way out (1 Cor. 10:13). Jesus completely understands every temptation we will ever face. God allows the temptations we face. But He will not allow anything beyond what we can endure if we trust Him. And, God has promised that there is a way out of every temptation. It may be hard. It may mean denying something pleasant. But God has given you everything you need to confess it, rebuke it, deny it, and dismiss it. And, He has given you His promised unconditional love and forgiveness every time you do fall for some tempting distraction. Tomas A Kempis wrote, *"We must not, therefore, despair when we are tempted but pray to God with so much the more fervor, that He may vouchsafe to help us in all tribulations, who, no doubt, according to the saying of St. Paul, will "make such issue with the temptation, that we may be able to bear it."* (1 Cor. 10:13). *Let us, therefore, humble our souls under the hand of God in all temptations and tribulations, for the humble in spirit He will save and exalt."* [29]

James reminds us that God doesn't change. God is the same now as He has always been. We can trust Him in the midst of our temptations. James says, ***"God chose to bring us to birth through His Word"*** (1:18a). Do you see how it's the opposite of what he just said temptation does? Evil desires that are not confessed, rebuked, denied, and dismissed get impregnated in our lives and give birth to the sin that distracts us form God, growing up into death. But, instead, to counteract that, God, impregnates us with His Word of truth, His very breath. And as we pay attention to that, instead of the temptations, His word gestates and comes to fruition as new life and strength in our lives. We can grow up to become what we are meant to be: more alive to God. We were created to be the pinnacle creature of God's creation, the agents within God's creation who consciously and responsively glorify God with our lives. We get to know, love, and serve God with our whole hearts, souls, minds, and strengths. And we get to lead creation in God's harvest of praise and service back to Him. James reminds us that we get to be the ***"firstfruits of all that God has created"*** (1:18b). This is what humanity is for. This is our mission. It's what God called Adam, and Israel, and the Church into. God's Word creates us, calls us, equips us, and commissions us to be His wise and mature Spiritual

---

[29] Kempis, Thomas A. Of the Imitation of Christ, trans. William Benham (Burlington: Inspirational Promotions, 1905), 20.

leaders in His mission of reconciling all things to Himself. We get to grow in being that. And God uses the challenges of the temptations in our lives to help us grow in that.

In the stories of the Desert Fathers, there is one of Abbot John the Dwarf. He prayed to God to take away all craving from his heart. His desires left him, and he became serine. When visiting another elder, he said, *"You see before you a man who is completely at rest and has no more temptations"*. The elder said, *"Go and pray to the Lord to command some struggle to be stirred up in you, for the soul is matured only in battles"*. He did. And when temptations started up again John did not pray that the struggles would be taken from him. Rather, he said, *"Lord, give me strength to get through the fight"*.

Let's pray.

> *Lord God, help us to recognize the distracting forces in our lives each day. Give us the wisdom to rebuke them, deny them, and dismiss them. And when we fail at these challenges, help us to remember your love and forgiveness. Help us to confess our distractions. Help us to see these temptations as opportunities to draw more closely to You. Open our hearts to return to you, to surrender back into your loving arms, and to receive your encouragement and renewal. Rebirth*

us back into Your mission – of knowing, loving, and serving You, Amen?

REFLECT:

What temptations have you faced lately?

How might these temptations be an invitation for you to grow?

How are you most tempted by power, pleasure, and passivity?

What might you need to confess, rebuke, deny, or dismiss?

How has God helped you out of temptations?

When did it feel like God was absent?

EXAMEN:

In quiet attention to God's loving presence, reflect on the challenges of temptations.

In gratitude, when have you been strengthened by facing temptations?

How are you feeling about temptations?

What is something about temptation that you can talk to God about?

What is something about temptations you can look forward to?

Seek God's guidance, help, and understanding. Pray about temptations.

EXERCISE:

Memorize these verses:

1 John 2:16   Heb. 4:15   Matt. 7:14   1 Cor. 10:13

Chapter 4

The Challenge of Listening

James 1:19-27

My dear friends take note of this: Everyone should be quick to listen and slow to speak. Be slow to become angry. A human being's passion does not bring about the righteous life that God desires. Therefore, as you continue to get rid of whatever stuff that is keeping you from hearing God's life giving Word, and continue to throw off whatever superfluous stuff that is keeping you from running freely in this life, then you can humbly submit to the Word God has planted in you, which brings you to wholeness. Don't just listen to God's instructions and erroneously think you've got it. No, you've got to put it into practice for it to be real. Anyone who just listens to God's Word without putting it into practice, is like someone ~~who~~ that sees themself in the mirror, but forgets what they looks like as soon as they walk away from the mirror. The one who looks deeply into God's perfect, freedom giving

revelation and does put it into practice, not
forgetting what they have heard, but doing it will be
blessed in the very practice of doing it. The Word
of life, which we humbly submit to, that God has
planted in you, which brings you to wholeness,
blesses us as we practice living it. If anybody
considers themselves to be truly religious, but
doesn't keep their own mouth in check, only
deceives themselves, and their religion is worthless.
The true religion that our Heavenly Father God
sees as pure and right is this: looking after orphans
and widows in need, and keeping oneself from being
distracted by the way of the world.

REALLY LISTENING

Most people have a story about getting in to trouble for not listening. One night Liz was telling me some things I needed to do the next day. Now, in my defense, it was 11 O'clock at night, and I was tired. She was saying, *"Oh, by the way, tomorrow you have got to do this, and this is going to happen, and remember to do this thing."* That's a paraphrase by the way. I was saying, *"Uh-huh. Yup. Uh-huh. Right."* It was all going in one ear and out the other. Then, the next day, I found myself with some rare free time in the afternoon. We had just moved to a new city, and I didn't have a lot of regular meetings happening yet. Suddenly I thought, *"I have got nothing going on right now. I've got about two hours here. This is so rare. I mean, I never have a block of two hours of time free. It's unbelievable. Well, I'm just going to sit down and read at Starbucks for about an hour"*. I sat there. It was so great, and I just had a great refreshing time, just by myself. Then I just took my time getting home. I walked in, and there's Liz. She was making dinner. She said, *"So, where's Rebekah?"* I said, *"Rebekah who?"* Then I remembered, Rebekah is our eldest. She was about six at this time. I said, *"Why are you asking me?"* Liz said, *"Remember last night, I said you need to pick up Rebekah from school today because her afterschool program is cancelled."* I said, *"No, I don't remember that."* Liz said, *"Well, I told you. And you replied. You said you would get her at 3 and now it's 5! Where is she?!"* I was terrified! I said, *"I don't know! I don't remember that conversation. I guess I*

69

wasn't listening." It was horrible. Do you know that horrible feeling of dread? Liz was looking at me, and I was so full of guilt for forgetting, and for wasting the last two hours, and I was imagining my daughter waiting at the school for me for two hours, or worse. Now, Liz had gotten a call at 3 when I didn't show up, and Rebekah had gone to a friend's house. Liz knew that and was just testing me. I was so relieved to find out she was OK. But it was a long time before I shook that horrible feeling of having abandoned my daughter. I will never forget to pick up my children again, and I haven't since.

It was a problem of not really listening. I have a great problem with that. I can hear it, but I'm not really listening. Even when it's not 11 at night, I can only take in a little bit at a time. Liz will say, *"Can you go and get me some butter from the store?"* I'll say, *"Sure."* But then she'll ad, *"Oh, and some milk".* Okay. Butter and milk, got it. But then she says the third one, broccoli. And I can't remember three things. Now I need a list. As soon as it goes beyond two things, I need a list, and I have to write it down. I can hear a third and fourth thing, but I can't retain it. Now at night, when she's telling me things, I say, *"Stop, wait, I have to write that down. Whatever you tell me right now, I will not remember".* And I'll get up and get a little pad of paper and start writing it all down.

PAYING ATTENTION

There are times when we may be hearing, but we're not listening. James says, *"My dear friends take note of this"*(1:19). I think he is referring back to the bridge verse before. He said, *"God chose to bring us to birth through His Word"* (1:18). God is speaking His Word into our lives. But we need to listen. We need to actually pay attention and truly hear and believe what God is saying. Sometimes we need to write it down to remember it. Then James ads, *"Everyone should be quick to listen and slow to speak"* (1:19). Being quick to listen and slow to speak is good advice. If you are listening to somebody and she is telling you something, be quick to listen and slow to speak. It's a good way to live. It's a good way of being a good friend, to listen and hold back on your advice. But I don't think that's necessarily what James is talking about here. I want us to remember the context.

What James is concerned about is spiritual formation, the spiritual work of God in us to move us towards spiritual wisdom and maturity. So when he says, *"therefore be quick to listen"*, we should ask, *"Listen to what?"* I think James is talking about being quick to listen to the Word of God, that Word which *"God chose to bring us to birth through"* (1:18). God is speaking His Word into our lives. It is the very breath of God that gives us life. You see, this is the context of the whole of James' letter. He wants us to be concentrating on paying attention to God's work in our lives. We need to be "quick" (ready, attentive, poised) to receive the life giving breath of God's Word. God's Word is recorded in the bible (2 Tim. 3:16, 17). God spoke to and through the Old Testament prophets and the New Testament apostles. Their words are the revelation of God for us. Jesus is God's Word made flesh (Heb. 1:1,2, John 1:14). He is the "visible expression of the invisible God" (Col. 1:15 JB Phillips). And, creation itself is Word of God (Gen. 1:1, Psalm 19, Rom. 1:18-20). God breathed out all of creation through His spoken Word. All of creation is an expression of Himself. All of creation is revealing God's praise and proclaiming His very nature. This is true of all the natural world, and it is also true of our own lives, our everyday experiences. Our existence is a part of God's creation. So, paying attention to God's Word includes paying attention to what is actually going on in your experiences; your thoughts, your feelings, your fears, your desires.

And, James says we need to be *"slow to speak"*. And we need to ask, *"Slow to speak what?"* I think he means slow to speak our own opinions. True spiritual life is a life of paying attention to God, not the lies of Satan. To give God "glory" means to pay attention to Him; to shine the light on Him, and listen to His revealing Word to us, not to glorify ourselves by paying so much attention to our own opinions about God. Many of these opinions come from the lies of Satan who means to confuse us with our fears and misconceptions of who God really is.

Then James ads a third directive. He says, *"**Be slow to become angry**"* (1:19). The Greek word for "angry" there is *"orgey"*. It's where we get the word "orgy." It can mean lust, or anger, or rage. But it can also mean passion or zeal. There is a righteous wrath that belongs to God, and we should hate what God hates. And there is a passion in our relationship with God that is good. But we have got to be careful in our wrath, careful in our passions. For *"**a human being's passion does not bring about the righteous life that God desires**"* (1:20). Human passion should not be confused with the righteousness of God. Just because we're passionate about something doesn't make it right. How much passion one demonstrates is not a test of how spiritual one is. Passion can lead to unbridled violence. Anger and rage can lead to fights, to conflict in families, and wars between nations. In fact, undisciplined passion, even Spiritual passion, even religious zeal, has been responsible for a lot of unrighteousness in the world. People have all this human passion, all this zeal for God, and they run off and do this and that for God. And sometimes we run off ahead of God, causing all kinds of havoc. We live in an age when we put so much emphasis on passion and zeal. I hear, *"Oh, it must be true. They must be good. That movement must be good; look at all the passion"*. I'm not as impressed with spiritual passion and zeal as I am with discipline and commitment. I don't really care that much about the passion. Show me the commitment. Show me the discipline. Show me the

Spiritual disciplines that build towards wisdom and maturity that lead towards a life of Spiritual transformation. I think that's what James is talking about here. Because people can get zealous and passionate, but when it disappears, they can disappear from the faith. That's what was going on in the church that James was overseeing. All the Jewish Christians had left Jerusalem. He's still in Jerusalem, but he cares about them. They have gone to all the corners of the earth. So he writes them this letter. What he cares about is not how zealous they are but how committed and disciplined they are to walk the walk of faith. So he implores them to be attentive to be paying attention to God's Word and to be slow in blabbing their own opinions, and slow to put much stock in fleeting passions. Stop and listen to God's Word. Be instructed. Grow in the slow process of wisdom and maturity.

Then James ads, **"Therefore, get rid of all (rhyparian) and the (perisseian kakias) that is so dominant"** (1:21a). Now, firstly (before I translate those Greek words!) remember, whenever there's a *"therefore"* we have to ask what is the "therefore" there for. I think James is saying, as you are quick to listen to God's word, slow to offer or believe your own opinions or theories, and as you patiently and carefully walk in the teaching and rebuking and correcting and training of God's word, get rid of two things.

PLUGGED UP EARS

This first one is *rhyparian*. The NIV translates it as "moral filth". Too often we too quickly reduce the Christian life to a moral improvement program, and we assume that this is what James is primarily talking about here. But there may be another way of hearing what James is talking about here. We find this word, *rhyparian* four times in the New Testament, and its literal meaning is "greasy, viscous, thick, sticky juice". In the common Greek language that James' contemporaries spoke and read, this word was most often used for earwax. That's its common meaning. Why might James use the literal word used for "earwax" for what he is talking about here? I think it makes perfect sense in the context of what he is talking about in the broader sense. This is the stuff that keeps us from hearing and being quick to listen to the Word of God.

I was dating a girl, and we were having dinner one time. And all through the meal, I kept saying, *"Huh? What? Huh? Excuse me? What?"* I couldn't hear her. She finally asked me if I was having trouble with my ears. I said, *"Well, actually, you know, I blew my nose the other day, and my ears went plugged; and I haven't been able to hear for, like, two days"*. She said, *"Have you ever had your ears cleaned?"* I asked her what she was talking about, and she explained that a doctor could do a procedure and clean your ears out at a clinic. I'd never heard of such a thing. So, right there in the middle of our date, we went to the clinic and asked for my ears to be washed out. The doctor sat me down. He put this kidney-shaped metal dish underneath my ear. Then he took this huge syringe and he pushed this hot water into my ear, and a big black thing came out. It hit the metal with a *"ping"*. I looked down and there was this *rhyparian*, right there, lying in that dish. And the moment that thing was out, I heard the doctor's clothes rustling. I hadn't been hearing people speak for a while, and suddenly I could clothes rustling. My hearing was repaired, and then I could understand, and apply all the messages that were being revealed to me. That's what James is talking about here, getting rid of the *rhyparian*, whatever it is that's plugging up your Spiritual ears and keeping you from really listening to God's Word. I love it when Greek words kind of sound like something in English we can associate the meaning with. You can think of *rhyparian* in association with "repair". We need repair. We need to get our ears fixed. They need to be unplugged so we can listen to the Word of God. This means taking the time and effort to actually pay attention to the study of what God is actually saying to us in His Word. It means taking time to read, study, meditate on, and memorize the Holy Scriptures.

TIED UP FEET

Likewise, the second problem is *perisseian kakias*, and it sounds like what it is in English. It is parasitic caca. The NIV translates it as "prevalent evil." The word literally means "bloodsucking badness", or "extra vice". This is all the stuff, or the things that keep us from actively walking the walk; putting God's Word into meaningful life practice. Years ago, we started an evening worship service for young people. The number of people attending grew very fast and we found ourselves crammed into a space that was way too small for us. So, we got rid of all the chairs and everyone just sat on the floor. When I was speaking one night, I was up against the front wall, and the first row was literally at my feet. My toes were touching the people in the front row. I could not take a step without stepping on someone. At the end of my message, I said a closing prayer. While I was praying, someone in the front row decided to tie my shoelaces together. After saying *"Amen"*, I attempted to move away from the front and, of course, I tripped into the audience to great laughter.

That's the picture here. What parasitical caca has your shoes all tied up? What is it that's keeping your feet from walking, walking the life of faith, walking the talk? What is it for you that are keeping you from clearly hearing the Word of God and putting it into active practice? What do you need to release yourself into disciplined walking with God? Do you need to start or keep regularly going to a good church? Do you need to join a home group? Do you need to join a bible study? Do you need to just simply pick up the bible and read God's Word? Do you need to go and buy some good commentaries? What is it that keeps you from hearing clearly, and what is it that is that caca that keeps you entangled? What kind of unhealthy relationship might you be in, or a habit that's hindering you? What lust? What greed? What gossip? What complaining? What laziness? What fear? What gluttony? What pride?

Remember the passage in Hebrew that says, *"Since we have this great company of witnesses surrounding us, let's get rid of all the stuff that hinders us (all that caca that so easily entangles us up), so we can run in this race that God has made us for with perseverance"* (Heb. 12:1, 2). We need hearing repair to hear God's instructions, and we need to get rid of parasitic caca that binds our feet. These are the two things James wants us to get rid of. We cannot be perfect in this life, but we can get rid of the earwax -- whatever prevents us from hearing God's word clearly -- and we can get rid of that parasitic caca that's in our life that entangles us.

There are some things that keep trapping you that you can just throw off. The good news is you don't have to do that thing anymore, whatever it is. You don't have to go to that place anymore. You don't have to visit that website again, or be in that relationship anymore, or be with those people again, or keep falling into that old habit again. You might need to get some help with other things that are persistent distractions. We all need help. I think everybody needs to be in some kind of 12-step program. We all need people around us who will support us, and we need to walk through the incremental steps of Spiritual formation. James is saying, **"Therefore, as you continue to get rid of whatever earwax that's keeping you from hearing God's life giving Word, and continue to throw off whatever superfluous caca that's keeping you from running freely in this life, then you can humbly submit to the Word**

God has planted in you, which brings you to wholeness" (1:21). James may be remembering the part of Jesus' Sermon on the Mount when the Lord recommended *"when you pray, do not be like the hypocrites, for they love to pray standing in the synagogues and on the street corners to be seen by men. I tell you the truth; they have received their reward in full. But when you pray, go into your room, close the door and pray to your Father, who is unseen. Then your Father, who sees what is done in secret, will reward you"* (Matt. 6:5, 6 NIV). Andrew Murray wrote: *"To follow Christ means that we must let go of excessive attachments to passing pleasures and possessions, to ploys of autonomous power, to tangible goods as if they were ultimate. Christ asks us to abandon our idols, whatever they may be, and to love Him with our entire being. "Pray to thy Father which is in secret." God is a God who hides Himself to the carnal eye. As long as in our worship of God we are chiefly occupied with our own thoughts and exercises, we shall not meet Him who is a spirit, the unseen One. But to the man who withdraws himself from all that is of world and man, and prepares to wait upon God alone, the Father will reveal Himself. As he forsakes and gives up and shuts out the world, and the life of the world, and surrenders himself to be led of Christ into the secret of God's presence, the light of the Father's love will rise upon him. The secrecy of the inner chamber and the closed door, the entire separation from all around us, is an image of, and so a help to that inner spiritual sanctuary, the secret of God's tabernacle, within the veil, where our spirit truly comes into contact with the Invisible One."*[30]

LISTENING AND DOING

We can't separate these two things: listening to God's Word and living the Spiritual life. The authentic Spiritual life is a life of listening and doing. We can't authentically have one without the other. We can't meaningfully do God's Word without continually listening to Him, and we can't listen to God's Word without actively living it into practice. That's the real challenge of hearing. We are not actually listening to God if we are not actually being transformed by the living Word of God. We are not actually listening to God if we are not seeing it being lived out in our everyday lives. James says, ***"Don't just listen to God's instructions and erroneously think you've got it. No, you've got to put it into practice for it to be real"*** (1:22). James uses a funny illustration to make his point. He says, ***"Anyone who just listens to God's Word without putting it into practice, is like a guy that sees himself in the mirror, but forgets what he looks like as soon as he walks away from the mirror"*** (1:23, 24). Imagine a guy looking at himself in the mirror. He stares at himself and thinks, *"OK. That's me. I know myself. I know the real me."* But, as soon as he walks away from the mirror he thinks, *"Wait. Was that me? What do I look like? Do I really know myself at all?"*

---

[30] Andrew Murray, *With Christ in the School of Prayer*, (Chicago: Donohue & Co., 1885), 26.

See, the Word of God is like a mirror. It shows us who really are, and more importantly who God really is, and who we really are in Christ. We can listen to God reveal reality to us through His Word. And, while we hear it, we can think, *"Yes. I get it. That's who God really is. That's who I really am. This is what I should really be and really do."* But, then, as we walk away, if we don't put it into real practice in everyday real life, it isn't real. It makes no sense. It is not imprinted on our daily reality. We quickly forget it, and begin to doubt it, and pretty soon we will scrap it all together.

The most sobering part of Jesus' Sermon on the Mount is when he said, *"Not everyone who says to me, 'Lord, Lord,' will enter the kingdom of heaven, but only he who does the will of my Father who is in heaven. Many will say to me on that day, 'Lord, Lord, did we not prophesy in your name, and in your name drive out demons and perform many miracles?' Then I will tell them plainly, 'I never knew you. Away from me, you evildoers!' Therefore everyone who hears these words of mine and puts them into practice is like a wise man who built his house on the rock. The rain came down, the streams rose, and the winds blew and beat against that house; yet it did not fall, because it had its foundation on the rock. But everyone who hears these words of mine and does not put them into practice is like a foolish man who built his house on sand. The rain came down, the streams rose, and the winds blew and beat against that house, and it fell with a great crash"* (Matt. 7:21-27 NIV).

You can read this part of James's letter, and say, *"Oh, yes, I get it, I get it, I get it."* But then, as you put the book down, get up, and walk away, it can all be gone. Unless you put it in to active practice, unless you really live as if it's really real, it will be gone. James is imploring us to not be the kind of people who hear God's Word without actually listening. Don't be like me hearing Liz tell me to pick up my daughter without actually hearing it. Write it down if your memory is as bad as mine is. Look deeply into the mirror of God's Word. Hear what He says about who you truly are: *an especially created, loved, saved, equipped, and sent one, on assignment from God on His mission.* Unplug your ears. Listen to the Word. Memorize it. Untangle you feet. Now run freely in the active living that God has revealed your reality to be. Make a commitment to believe God's Word by putting it into active practice.

James contrasts the person who hears without putting into practice, with the one **"who looks deeply into God's perfect, freedom giving revelation and does put it into practice, not forgetting what he has heard, but doing it"**. James says that person will, **"be blessed in the very practice of doing it."** (1:25). You are blessed in practicing this life of freedom in Christ. You get to continually listen to God speaking through His recorded Word (the bible), and through your conscience which He has created and informed, and through the Holy Spirit, who is in you and acts as your freedom life-coach, calling out reminders, and warnings, and encouragements, and through your wise and mature brothers and sisters in Christ, and through the daily experiences of God meeting you in His creation.

We have our opinions about God, but have our opinions about God been shaped by the revealed truth of God's Word? We have our frameworks that guide our theological perspectives about God and reality. But have we let the honest hearing of God's Word continually reshape our theological frameworks? That's one of the great things that happens as we study God's Word and see who God really; see what the gospel really is, and find out who we really are. Our opinions get reshaped, and God's truth gets implanted in us more. Have you really heard the good news? Have you really heard that God loves you so much it hurt; that there is nothing you could ever do to cause God to love you any more than he loves you right now; that there is nothing you could ever do to cause God to love you any less than he loves you right now; that he offers you a free gift of absolute forgiveness and eternal life; that he has done everything that the righteous law requires for you already through the life, death, and resurrection and ascension of Jesus Christ; that you only need to receive the free gift by believing it through faith, and you are saved; but just as good of news that you are called and equipped into his service to be an agent of reconciliation, to extend the love of God in this world? That's the Word of truth that gives us Spiritual birth. That's *the Word of life that we humbly submit to that God has planted in you, which brings you to wholeness*

(1:21). That's the *"perfect, freedom giving revelation ... (which)* *blesses us as we practice living it"* (1:25).

PUT IT INTO PRACTICE

Have you really heard it? Have you really listened to it? Are you really paying attention to the voice of God's Holy Spirit in your life? Are you really living it into the active reality of your life? We get to listen to God's Word every Sunday at church services. We get to listen to God's Word read, sung, prayed, and preached. We get to listen to God's Word every day in personal devotions and study. We get to listen to God's Word through out the week together. Today we can listen to the very best bible teaching ever recorded on sites through the Internet. But, we have got to put it into action. We have got to let Him penetrate us with His truth, to enlighten us and convict us and rebuke us and correct us and lead us. Then we have to go and live it, putting it into active practice.

When a woman, hearing Jesus' teaching, yelled from the crowd, *"Blessed is the woman who gave birth to you!"* Jesus replied, *"Actually, blessed are the ones who hear the Word of God and put it into practice"* (Luke 11:27, 28). Likewise, the Apostle Paul said, *"It's not the ones who just hear the law who are in a right in God's view, but it's the ones who actually practice it who will be called right with God"* (Rom. 2:13). You know, it's like money; it only grows as it's invested. It's like a skill. It's only as it is practiced that it gets developed. It's like a sponge. It is only as it gets squeezed out that it can get filled up again.

Jesus and Paul agree with James. If you think that a mere outward show of religious ceremony is the actual grace-filled life, you are only deceiving yourself because you are not impressing God, and you are probably not impressing anybody else either. James continues, *"If anybody considers themselves truly religious, but doesn't keep their own mouth in check, that one deceives themselves, and their religion is worthless"* (1:26). I believe he's referring back to the idea of being quick in listening to God's Word, and slow in the speech and passions of one's own opinions. He's saying, that if people think they're faithfully doing what God desires but they can't practice being quick to listen to God's Word, being slow to give or believe their own or the world's opinions about God, and being patient and careful in their passions and their zeal, then they're only fooling themselves, because God is certainly not fooled, and neither are most people watching them.

Psalm 149 prays:

> *Set a guard over my mouth, O Lord,*
> *keep watch over the door of my lips.*
> *Let not my heart be drawn to what is evil,*
> *to take part in wicked deeds*
> *with people who are evildoers;*
> *let me not eat of their delicacies.*

But my eyes are fixed on you, O Sovereign Lord.

In you I take refuge.

Do not give me over to death.

Keep me from the snares they have laid for me

from the traps set by evildoers.

Let the wicked fall into their own nets

while I pass by in safety.

Isn't that good? That's a promise of God, that we get to unplug our ears and we get to walk in safety, unentangled, with the Spirit's help. Let's go and do that this week. If you are stuck right now, though, if there's something that is plugging up your ears so you can't hear, and there's something entangling your feet so you can't walk – reach out to God for help. Call on a wise Christian friend or pastor to get some help to walk in the freedom God wants for you.

SOLITUDE AND SILENCE

Another important discipline for keeping one's *"mouth in check"* is practicing the spiritual disciplines of solitude and silence. This is the habit of taking time away to be alone, away from the usual distractions that bombard us. Finding a quiet place, and being completely silent in isolated reflection is an important exercise for spiritual development. Henri Nouwen wrote, *"In solitude we can slowly unmask the illusion of our possessiveness and discover in the center of our own self that we are not what we can conquer, but*

86

what is given to us. In solitude we can listen to the voice of him who spoke to us before we could speak a word, who healed us before we could make any gesture to help, who set us free long before we could free others, and who loved us long before we could give love to anyone. It is in this solitude that we discover that being is more important than having, and that we are worth more than the result of our efforts. In solitude we discover that our life is not a possession to be defended, but a gift to be shared. It's there we recognize that the healing words we speak are not just our own, but are given to us; that the love we can express is part of a greater love, and that the new life we bring forth is not a property to cling to, but a gift to be received." [31]

James sums up this invitation to reflect on the challenge of hearing by saying, ***"The true religion that our Heavenly Father God sees as pure and right is this: looking after orphans and widows in need, and keeping oneself from being distracted by the way of the world"*** (1:27). James's original Hebrew Christian audience would have caught this phrase about "widows and orphans" as the most basic action of God's way. They would have recognized this from Isaiah 1 and Psalm 82. They knew Jesus had repeated it in Matthew 25. This is shorthand for the most basic way of practicing the grace filled, Spiritual life. It's in the down-to-earth, everyday things of life that the Spiritual life is put into action. As Jesus said in His Sermon

---

[31] Henri Nouwen, *Out of Solitude: Three Meditations on the Christian Life*, (Notre Dame: Ava Maria Press, 1974), 25, 26.

on the Mount: *"Be careful not to do your 'acts of righteousness' before men, to be seen by them. If you do, you will have no reward from your Father in heaven. So when you give to the needy, do not announce it with trumpets, as the hypocrites do in the synagogues and on the streets, to be honored by men. I tell you the truth, they have received their reward in full. But when you give to the needy, do not let your left hand know what your right hand is doing, so that your giving may be in secret. Then your Father, who sees what is done in secret, will reward you"* (Matt. 6:1-4 NIV).

It's not primarily in the spectacular, passionate acts of ear-plugged, foot-stuck, tongue wagging that are the expressions of real Spiritual wisdom and maturity. It is the everyday actions of disciplined love and sacrifice, justice and mercy, humility and generosity that are true Christian Spirituality. These are the invitations to "hear" the Word of God. Who is the widow or the orphan in your world, in your life, to whom you can show humble mercy and justice to today? It's in these simple acts of living God's grace and mercy that we experience God changing us. And these are the daily invitations to truly listen to and trust in God.

Let's pray.

God, we confess that so often we have heard Your Word, we have read Your Word, and it can become just like a noise to us, a babbling, and we haven't really heard You in it. God, we confess that. But today we give You our attention anew, and we give

You this commitment, this vow, that we will not just hear Your Word. We want to really hear it, and we want to really put it into practice. So, God, bring to mind, by Your Holy Spirit, maybe that one thing, that one thing that we need to do to get rid of that earwax; that one thing we need to do to get rid of whatever is entangling us and keeping us from walking the walk. Lord, help us as we walk through our days, that we wouldn't be like those who looked in the mirror and forgot who they are. God, help us to remember what You have said. Remind us all week of whom You are and whom we are and how we get to serve You. God, we pray, trusting in your mercy, that you will do these things so that we can know, love, and serve You better. Amen?

REFLECT:

How are you doing with listening?

When has someone spoken to you but you didn't really hear them?

When have you felt like someone didn't really hear you?

How might your ears be plugged?

How might your feet be tied?

EXAMEN:

In quiet attention to God's loving presence, reflect on the challenges of listening.

In gratitude, when have you been strengthened by listening?

How are you feeling about listening?

What is something about listening that you can talk to God about?

What is something about listening you can look forward to?

Seek God's guidance, help, and understanding. Pray about listening.

EXERCISE:

Practice a solitude and/or silent retreat.

Try to pay attention to what God is saying to you.

Journal what God may be teaching you.

Chapter 5

The Challenge of Discrimination

James 2:1-13

Friends, as the ones who trust in our exalted master, Jesus Christ, we don't discriminate between people. Imagine if one person shows up to your gathering wearing gold jewelry and nice clothes, and another person shows up wearing grubby clothes. If you give preferential treatment to the one wearing fine clothes, saying, "Here's a special seat for you" but say to the grubby one, "You stand over there" or "Sit on the floor by my feet" aren't you practicing discrimination and judgmentalism with evil intent? Pay attention, my dear friends. It's so like God to choose those who are insignificant in the world's perspective to be significant in the faith perspective, and to give them the riches of the Kingdom that He has promised those who love Him. But you discriminate against the poor, even though the rich (whom you exalt) are the very ones who are manipulating you. They're the ones who are exploiting you in the court system. They're the ones who are offending the integrity of the way of Jesus to whom you belong. If you are really keeping the way of the Kingdom found in bible ("Love your neighbor as yourself") you are getting it right. If you discriminate, you're getting it wrong, and you're condemning yourself. Keeping the Law, but missing this crucial bit is to miss the whole thing. For the one who commanded, "Do not commit adultery", also commanded, "Do not murder". If you do not commit adultery but you do commit murder, you are still a lawbreaker. Speak and act like those who live in way of grace that gives freedom, because discrimination without grace will be experienced by anyone who doesn't practice love and mercy. Mercy triumphs over discrimination.

The next invitation to examine the maturity of our faith that James addresses is the challenge of discrimination. How we treat other people is a demonstration of how much we understand and are living in the way of the good news of Jesus Christ. We could alternatively call this the challenge of judgment, or snobbery, or grace, or mercy. James starts the second chapter of his letter by saying, *"Friends, as the ones who trust in our exalted master, Jesus Christ, we don't discriminate between people"* (2:1). He states it as a fact. People who serve Jesus (the only exalted one) don't discriminate between any one. We are all equal under Jesus. That word for "discrimination" (or "favoritism" in the NIV) is *"pros-oro-leempsia"*. It is a three part compound word. *"Pros"* is to face something, or someone. *"Oro"* (from *horos*) is to look, or gaze at something or someone. And, *"leempsia"* (from *lambano*) is to select, or take, or receive something or someone. *Prosoroleempsia* means to judge by appearance, to distinguish between, and accept or reject people, based on what they look like.

Apparently this was as serious a problem in the Early Church as it is today. We know from the letters of the New Testament that the first Christians dealt with the very human propensity to discriminate between people. The Early Church was a radically diverse community. It included people of diverse economic status. Slaves, free people, merchants, and ruling class folks all met together for worship and fellowship. All genders participated equally. There were a multitude of races mixing together. People of different cultures engaged in common meals and each other's customs. People spoke many different languages. Paul even encouraged having interpreters on hand to enable understanding among a multitude of "foreign tongues (language speakers)" (1 Cor. 14). There were a variety of different life-styles. Sometimes these customs clashed, as some members practiced behaviors that other members considered unconscionable (1 Cor. 8, 10). They came from many assorted cultures with many opposing customs. They probably had their own versions of the worship music wars! But, consistently throughout the New Testament, the test of whether Church people were practicing the authentic way of Jesus Christ, was whether they were treating people without discrimination while navigating all these common differences. The authentic way of Jesus is the way of unconditional love for everyone. That means every person is honored and respected in spite of their differences. In fact, in the authentic way of Jesus, these differences are meant to be celebrated not circumvented. They are invitations to practice the extravagantly accommodating love of God.

SHAMEFUL ACTS

This is a uniquely Christian perspective. At their best, the practices of diversity among the Christians of the first century were a cause of scandal among the pious Romans, Greeks, and Jews. Throughout the New Testament we see the evidence of Christians being misunderstood and discriminated against, sometimes for their inclusion of women, sinners, Greeks, or young people in Christian community (Luke, 9, 24, Matt. 9, 11, Acts 16, 17, 18, 21, Mark 10, 1 Tim. 4:12). By 64AD Christians were being persecuted under Emperor Nero, often being scapegoated for their peculiar distinctives. Pliny the Younger (governor of Bithynia in 111AD) wrote to Emperor Trajan about Christians' *"shameful acts"* (sections 7-10). The Roman historian Tacitus (c. 115AD) complained of Christians' *"anti-social beliefs"* (Annals 15.44). And the Roman historian Suetonius (c. 121AD) complained about Christians' *"disturbance"*, *"new and mischievous superstition"*, and *"excessive religiosity"* (Nero, 16, Lives of the Twelve Caesars). Early Christians were noted for their scandalous lack of discrimination, being mocked for their "shameful" associations with slaves, women, the poor, and the undesirable.

We tend to have the opposite situation in most of our churches today. We have a hard time not morphing into homogeneous communities of like-minded, like-skinned, like-life-styled people. We fracture into smaller and smaller categories of similarity, and then develop xenophobic judgments about anyone who is a little different. Meanwhile, we tend to favor people who are like us, or who are like what we wish we were like. Further, we tend to exalt people for all the wrong reasons: what they look like, what they sound like, their talents, their wealth (even if it was dishonorable gained). That's the real "shameful acts" scenario.

PREFERENTIAL TREATMENT

James is making the point, that only Jesus is exalted. Everyone else is on the same plain together under God. Partiality is inconsistent with the way of Jesus. Our partiality in treating people differently is an opportunity to examine just how unaligned with the way of Jesus we may yet be. James uses an example from every day life to show how discrimination works. He says, *"Imagine if one man shows up to your gathering wearing gold jewelry and nice clothes, and another man shows up wearing grubby clothes"* (2:2). James is painting a scene from a church meeting. Two different people show up. One is obviously rich. He has all the outward privilege and dignity of wealth. The other is a dirty beggar. Imagine that scene. What are your first thoughts when you see each of these people? What are your assumptions? What are your feelings? How do you interact with each of them?

James says, *"If you give preferential treatment to the one wearing fine clothes, saying, "Here's a special seat for you," but say to the grubby one, "You stand over there" or "Sit on the floor by my feet," aren't you practicing discrimination and judgmentalism with evil intent?"* (2:3, 4). The word he uses for "preferential treatment" is *"epi blepo"* which means, "extra looking at". We tend to give extra attention to those who we find outwardly attractive. I remember preaching at our church and being distracted by someone in the front row. He looked so familiar. He was also very hansom, fit, and well dressed. He also was sitting with a very attractive woman. After the service I noticed that a large group of men had surrounded this guy. Later someone told me who he was. He was a famous hockey star. Now, this was in Canada, and no one gets more attention than successful hockey stars!

We also tend to avoid those we find physically repulsive. The context for James' example is a church meeting. Some people have experienced the worst of human discrimination in church settings. Sadly, some people avoid churches because they know they will be discriminated against. One person said, *"Church? Why would I go there? I already feel bad about myself. Why would I go somewhere where they make me feel worse about myself?"* Let's admit: Some people are more attractive than others. We get mesmerized by those who look good. We want to look at them more. And we want to associate with those who are more attractive, partly because we want to BE one of the more attractive people. We wish people would look at us with that kind of mesmerizing attention. But all of this attraction is based on what's on the outside: looks, clothes, talents, stuff. We give too much attention to one person *("sit here" – you're special)*, and not enough attention to another *("stand over there" – you're a looser)*. Or worse, we inflate ourselves above another *("sit at my feet"- because I'm one of the important people*). These are not Spiritual values.

DESPERATE TO FEEL VALUED

We are so desperate to be admired and feel valued and significant. We all want to be one of the important people. There is an interesting common human experience of a life cycle of searching for significance. We start as children with no autonomy. We are nobodies, completely dependent on others for care and consequence. As our bodies develop we gain independence. We also compare ourselves to others to know our places in the attraction pecking order. We begin our drive for personal self-worth through acquiring the right toys, clothes, hairstyles, music, accomplishments and experiences. Soon we look to making money to gain more independence and significance. We collect titles and degrees, cars and careers, family and fame, achievements and accolades. We hope to be important people. Then, as we age, we begin to loose all the things that give us significance. We loose our careers, our young bodies, our families and friends, until at last, we find ourselves back in a position of lacking autonomy, being cared for by others, becoming nobodies again, completely dependent on others for care and consequence. It is interesting that the invitation to wisdom and maturity, as one ages, is an invitation to slowly lose all of the outwardly attractive things of this world.

We learn at a young age that there are important people and unimportant people. My Dad would often make a comment about someone saying, *"He's got an important job"*. We learn to put people on pedestals because they have earned some kind of greater substance. But, then we dismiss them when they disappoint us by being too mortal after all. We get very excited about celebrities in our culture. Even in our churches, we can fall for the cults of the celebrity Christian, the person from the big church in the big city, or the outside expert. We are really only impressed by these people because we don't really know them. Blinded by the inflated allure of these "important" people, we miss the inherent value of each unique, individual, regular person. It is only as we truly get to know people that we come to appreciate the true heroism of individual lives; especially those who have acquired true wisdom and maturity, the true beauty of real goodness and depth.

James' point is that there's no discrimination in the Kingdom of God. We are all equal in Christ. We have the same value, but we are all unique. The word James uses for "discrimination" here is *"diakrino"*. It means to elevate one and condemn another. It is always based on worldly categories with which we compare and compete, diminish and dismiss. Isn't that ***"practicing discrimination and judgmentalism with evil intent"?*** (2:4). James says we have made ourselves out to be "judges". The word here is *"kirinai"*. It means to pass sentence on and condemn. And we do it with "evil intent" (*ponero dialogismo*). Ultimately, all this comparing, competing, and condemning is from an evil place that is far from the way of Jesus.

I experienced discrimination recently. I was looking for a new job and was in the process of applying to several churches for pastoral positions. Over a period of about two years I was in contact with about thirteen different churches. During this process, I heard the exact same phrase from five different people from four different churches. They each said, *"We are looking for a young man with a young family"*. One other person, from a church that did not hire me was telling me about the person they did hire saying, *"Isn't it great, now all three of our pastors are under forty!"* Now, I knew that this is a common sentiment, but I did tell a few of these people, *"I know you are thinking that, but don't say it out loud. That's illegal!"* That is ageism and it is illegal to not hire people because of their age. It is also dumb to disqualify them for employment because they may have so much more wisdom and experience than someone else. That is discrimination. Now I know that this is a fraction of what others have suffered in being discriminated against. But everyone's suffering is suffering to them, and is experienced as pain to them.

DISCRIMINATING VS DISCERNING

Now, we need to clarify that there is a difference between discriminating and discerning. Discrimination condemns people because of some outward appearances. Discernment holds all people to standards of good and bad character and behavior. There is a difference between being judgmental and judging. Judgmentalism condemns people as worthless. Judgment makes critical distinctions between what is worthy and unworthy of our attention. There is a difference between a critical mind and a critical heart. A critical heart can never see anything good. A critical mind can recognize the difference between what is good and what is not. Discrimination, judgmentalism, and critical hearts are not the Jesus way. Discernment, judgment, and a critical mind are vital to the Jesus way. Oswald Chambers wrote, *"When we discern that people are not going on spiritually and allow the discernment to turn to criticism, we block our Way to God. God never gives us discernment in order that we may criticize, but that we may intercede"*.[32]

In The Sermon on the Mount, Jesus warns against the dangers of living by discrimination. He said, *"Do not condemn or dismiss people, or you too will be condemned and dismissed. For in the same way that you condemn or dismiss others, you will be condemned and dismissed. You'll experience the same diminishment you give out to others"* (Matt. 7:1, 2). We may be quick to condemn or dismiss others. Often the things we most condemn others for are the very things we are most ashamed of in our selves. We live under such heavy self-condemnation. Then, in our shame, we project that

---

[32] Oswald Chambers, *My Utmost for His Highest* (Uhrichville: Barbour Publishing, 1963), 329.

self-hatred on to others. In this way we try to elevate ourselves by condemning and diminishing others. All of this is because we are so desperate to be admired and feel valued and significant, to be one of the important people.

YOU'RE A WINNER!

I have some really good news! You don't need to impress anyone. You already have the greatest significance imaginable. First, do you realize that you won a race against about one hundred million others just to be born? You were the one sperm that won that race to be the first one to cross the finish line and break that barrier to fertilize that egg to win your conception. You beat out those 400 million others just to be born. You are a born winner! You were also selected to be adopted into the family of God. God has chosen to adopt you as His child. You were picked out of the orphanage of obscurity and welcomed into the palace of your father the King. You belong to the family of the King, and you've been given full membership and inheritance of the royal family. You are a part of that famous family. You have also been given the deposit of the presence of God's Holy Spirit living in you. He is your priceless resource and personal guide at all times. He will never leave you, and He will equip you with everything you need at every step of your life, and He will guide you in every area of your life. And, you have been commissioned with the most important job that any human being has ever had. You are an ambassador of God. You might talk with someone and ask, *"What's your job?"* Maybe he will say, *"I'm the President of the United States."* And you can say, *"Well, good for you. That's nice. But I am the ambassador for the King of the Universe".* That's the most important job there is. So, you have no need to ever seek anyone's approval or appreciation again.

If we can reimagine our own self-worth in relation to whom God has declared us to be, rather than engaging in the competitive and condemning chaos of the world's way, maybe we can give others the same consideration in the Jesus way. It's the right-side-up Kingdom way of thinking about others and ourselves. James says, ***"Pay attention, my dear friends: Isn't this so like God, to choose those who are insignificant in the world's perspective to be significant in the faith perspective, and to inherit the riches of the Kingdom which he has promised those who love him?"*** (2:5). God has decided to use the seemingly insignificant people of this world to demonstrate His true significance. The apostle Paul urges his friends in Corinth to recall their true significance. He says, *"Remember what you were when you were called. Not many of you were wise by human standards; not many were influential; not many were of noble birth. But God chose the foolish things of the world to shame the wise; God chose the weak things of the world to shame the strong. He chose the lowly things of this world and the despised things — and the things that are not — to nullify the things that are, so that no one may boast before him"* (1 Cor. 1:26-29 NIV).

In the right-side-up Kingdom of God, the seemingly insignificant people of the world are actually the rich ones, while the world's rich are the poor ones. The early Church was made up primarily of those who were not wealthy or powerful. But they were rich in faith and heirs of the Kingdom. Now, we must be careful not to sanctify the "poor" just because they are poor. They are not blessed because they are poor. Nor are the rich excluded from the Kingdom because they are rich. No matter what one's circumstances are, if one is "in Christ", one is rich in the Kingdom and that's what really matters.

EXPLOITATION AND CORRUPTION

But, James reminds us that we so easily turn things wrong way up. Using the example of the ways we discriminate according to worldly wealth, he says, *"But you discriminate against the poor, even though the rich (whom you exalt) are the very ones who are manipulating you. They're the ones who are exploiting you in the court system. They're the ones who are offending the integrity of the way of Jesus to whom you belong"* (2:6, 7). We keep cow towing to the rich, even as they exploit us and demean us. We do this to get their favor because we all wish we were one of them.

But this is corrupt. The systems that keep some in affluence, while others in poverty are rigged for the rich and discriminate against the poor. One unjust way of exploiting the poor is through court systems, or any structure that favors those with lots of resources. To favor people because of their wealth, social status, or worldly power is "offending" (*blasphemousin* – literally blaspheming insulting, slandering, cursing) *the integrity* (the very name) *of the way of Jesus to whom you belong*" In contrast, the way of God is the way of justice: "*This is what the LORD Almighty says: 'Administer true justice; show mercy and compassion to one another. Do not oppress the widow or the fatherless, the alien or the poor. In your hearts do not think evil of each other'* (Zech. 7:9, 10 NIV). If we belong to Jesus, we will be about His justice. That will mean combating the injustices of any kind of discrimination.

NO DISCRIMINATION HERE!

In fact, James says, **"If you are really keeping the way of Kingdom found in bible ("Love your neighbor as yourself") you are getting it right"** (2:8). True justice and faith is loving everyone unconditionally. There is no discrimination in the Kingdom of God. There's no room for any worldly distinctions between those who are deemed to be worthy and those who are not. There's no room for any distinction between those who are typically deemed to be attractive and those who are not. Love overlooks any worldly distinctions between people. Imagine if one of your own children became wealthier than the others – would you love them more or less? Of course not! Love overlooks any superficial distinctions between people. And love shows respect and kindness to all - even in spite of some personally distasteful things. **"But"**, James says, **"if** *you discriminate, you're getting it wrong, and you're condemning yourself"* (2:9). To show any "favoritism" (NIV) is to break the very Law of the Kingdom. It is to miss the point of the Kingdom. And, James warns us, *"Keeping the Law, but missing this crucial bit is to miss the whole thing"* (2:10). Here James is again referring to Jesus' Sermon on the Mount. Throughout that sermon, Jesus said, *"You've heard it said (do this or that) ... but I say (here's the point of why we do this or that)"*. And, in the end the point is: to love God with your whole heart, soul, mind, and strength, and to love your neighbor as yourself. If we are discriminating against anyone, we are missing the point of the whole thing. This is a crucial test of the true character of our faith.

EMPATHY

Real love involves unconditional acceptance of another person. It doesn't mean we necessarily agree with any of their ideas or actions. But it does mean that we truly empathize with them. Empathy means one feels and appreciates another's point of view. Empathy is the most important tool we have in human interaction. There is no love without actual empathy. This is why I love to read fiction. Good fiction is an opportunity to enter the world of others. It is an emersion in the stories of other people's thoughts, feelings, experiences, hopes, mistakes, sins, joys, and fears. It is interesting that most of our bible is story. Most of the Holy Scriptures is not moral instruction, but the life stories of real people interacting with the real God. It's like God said, *"I want to help you understand the Spiritual life. But instead of giving you a lecture, let me tell you some stories"*. Then He invites us in to empathically engage with Adam and Eve, Abraham and Sarah, Moses and Miriam, Joshua and Rahab. And not just the "good guys", He also invites us into the life stories of Lot and his daughters, Jonah and his whale, Ahab and Jezebel, Judas and Pilot. And if we are really paying attention, we see that there are no "good guys" and "bad guys" in the bible. There are just people – like you and me; every one of whom is making daily decisions to either respond to God's invitation of life, or turning away from God in subtle or overt ways.

We recently finished a twenty-week study of the life of David in our church. It was very difficult for many people to see the point. People kept asking, *"What's the point here? What am I supposed to get out of this? Am I supposed to go fight Philistines? I don't know any! Am I supposed to marry several people at once? Am I supposed to fight a literal giant, or go hide in a cave?"* And, of course, the point is not to reduce God's biblical revelation to an encyclopedia of morality. The point is to enter into the story. Get into the story. And even better: Let the story get in to you; to see yourself in the grand story of God creating, saving, and calling each of us into His story. A wonderful thing about stories is that we get to see results of engaging rightly and wrongly with God without having to experience the horrible consequences ourselves. We don't have to get swallowed by a whale. We can see from Jonah's experience how awful that is and choose to obey God in the first place instead. We all have these choices of how we will respond. Will we respond in grateful engagement, or in subtle and overt ways reject the invitation and ignore God and our place in His story?

IT'S YOUR CHOICE

We have a choice: To live by the world's standards, rules, and view of things (which leads to death), or to live by the Kingdom's standards, rules, and view of things (which leads to life). We live by one or the other. Though God's truth, love, and beauty is everywhere in God's created world, it takes a spiritual mind to discern them from the many imitations. One of the tests of which way we are living is the way we treat people. You can't think you are meeting the requirements of the law if you keep only some of it. Jesus went through the Ten Commandments in His Sermon on the Mount (Matt. 5:17-48). He pointed out that the whole Law is summed up in Loving God (Commandments 1 – 4) and people (Commandments 5-10). It's about truly loving God with one's whole heart, soul, mind, and strength, and loving one's neighbor as one's self. And, truly loving God and people means not objectifying them. It's not about technically fulfilling the letter of the Law. It's about fulfilling the Spirit of the Law – truly loving God and others. James says, *"For the one who commanded, "Do not commit adultery," also commanded, "Do not murder." If you do not commit adultery but you do commit murder, you are still a lawbreaker"* (2:11). Some people might be proud to have never been a murderer or an adulterer, but by discriminating amongst people by any outward appearance is to be just as guilty as a murderer or adulterer. So, James says, **"Speak and act like those who live under in way of grace which gives freedom, because discrimination without grace will be experienced by anyone who doesn't practice love and mercy. Mercy triumphs over discrimination"** (2:12, 13).

We have a choice: live by standards of discrimination and condemnation with no mercy, or live by the perspective of grace and love for all. You are freely loved and forgiven - so freely love and forgive. This is a test of how closely we are following the way of Jesus. The apostle Paul urged the Philippians to *"do nothing out of selfish ambition or vain conceit, but in humility consider others better than yourselves. Each of you should look not only to your own interests, but also to the interests of others. Your attitude should be the same as that of Christ Jesus: Who, being in very nature God, did not consider equality with God something to be grasped, but made himself nothing, taking the very nature of a servant, being made in human likeness. And being found in appearance as a man, he humbled himself and became obedient to death — even death on a cross!"* (Phil. 2:3-8 NIV).

Let's pray.

Dear God, we acknowledge that in our guilt and shame we have poured contempt on others with awful discrimination. We have judged others and exalted ourselves. We have not humbly acknowledged the grace you have given to us and to others. We have idolized the rich and famous, even as they exploit us and demean us. We recommit ourselves to your service, and to your mercy, and justice, and love of all. Help us to better appreciate each human being as your uniquely created, called, equipped and commissioned one. Help us to pay attention to the ways we treat others and to see how we may grow in practicing the way of Jesus among any people you bring us along side of. Amen?

REFLECT:

How are you doing with discrimination?

What kind of people are you honestly uncomfortable being around?

What kinds of people scare you?

Who do you know who is very different from you?

When have you felt discriminated against?

EXAMEN:

In quiet attention to God's loving presence, reflect on the challenges of discrimination.

In gratitude, when have you been strengthened by empathy?

How are you feeling about discrimination?

What is something about discrimination that you can talk to God about?

What is something about discrimination you can look forward to?

Seek God's guidance, help, and understanding. Pray for empathy.

EXERCISE:

Try sitting with someone at church who is very different from you.

Invite someone different from you to a meal.

Read something from a very different point of view from your own.

Practice simply listening to an other person's ideas without arguing.

Chapter 6

The Challenge of Actions

James 2:14-26

What does it gain us friends, if we claim to believe but
don't put our belief into practice? Imagine seeing
your brother or sister naked or hungry. If you say
them, "Go in peace. Be warm. Be fed", but you
don't give them anything practical to supply their
needs, what use is that? Likewise, faith alone without
practical action is dead. But, someone might say,
"You have faith, and I have actions". Try to show me
faith without actions! Instead, I'll show you my faith
through my actions. You believe there is one God.
Well, that's good. But even demons believe that –
and tremble! Do you want proof, you dummy, that
faith without practical action is useless? How about
old Abraham? Didn't he prove he believed when he
offered up Isaac on the alter? Can you see that his
faith and his practice worked together? His practice
completed his faith. And, the Scripture says,
"Abraham actively trusted God, and that proved his

faith". And he was called "a friend of God". See?
It's through practicing faith that one is called faithful,
not just through believing alone. Likewise, wasn't
Rahab, the prostitute called faithful because of her
actions when she hid those spies and sent them safely
off? She was called faithful because of her actions.
Just like a body without breath is dead, so faith
without practical actions is dead.

PROVE IT!

It's easy to say you love someone. It's far harder to prove it. One could argue that love is a verb, and can only be real when it can be demonstrated. One Mother's day I tried to organize a whole Sunday afternoon of many things that my wife, Liz loves. I began the afternoon by dropping her at a beach with our kids because she loves our kids and the outdoors. Meanwhile, I drove to the next spot to arrange the next event in a string of experiences for her. By the end of the day I was exhausted, but very proud of myself for making it such a great day for her. But, later, I noticed that she did not seem happy. I asked her if she had enjoyed the day. She pensively replied, "*Sort of*". I was dumb struck! I had worked so hard on that whole day's events! Then she explained that she was disappointed that I had spent the day running around arranging events, rather than being with her. As I dumbly stared at her, she asked, "*Do you even know what my love language is?*" Now, you have to appreciate that Liz and I regularly give seminars on marriage enrichment and one of the great tools is Gary Chapman's book, 'The Five Love Languages'. But, at that moment I could not even name one of the love languages, let alone Liz's. I lamely said, "*The talking one?*" I meant, 'spending time together'. That's one of the actual five, and it's Liz's love language. Instead of spending time with her, I had arranged a series of events for her without me. A love language is the way someone actually feels love. It's the way you show your love to that person. It's usually not your own language, so if you really love someone, you learn their love language and demonstrate your love to them by conveying your love for them in that way. It's a way you "prove" your love. Ironically, Liz knocked it out of the park one 'Father's Day' when she spent money we didn't have to buy me my fist laptop computer. I knew that she was sacrificing her own dislike of spending money to "prove" how much she loves me by getting me that incredible gift. This is the challenge of actions.

James says, *"What does it gain us friends, if we claim to believe but don't put our belief into practice?"* (2:14). *"Imagine"*, He says, *"You see your brother or sister naked or hungry. If you say them, "Go in peace. Be warm. Be fed", but you don't give them anything practical to supply their needs, what use is that?"* (2:15, 16). Can you imagine doing that? Can you imagine meeting your own brother or sister on the street, and they are naked and hungry. You cheerily say, *"Feel good! Be warm! Be fed!"* and then you keep walking by without actually doing anything tangible to actually clothe or feed them. What if someone asked your naked and hungry brother or sister if they believed you loved them? What would they say? They'd probably say, *"No! Those words were useless!"* James says, *"Likewise, faith alone without practical action is dead"* (2:17).

FAITH VS ACTIONS

Now, James anticipates someone's defense. He says, *"But, someone might say, "You have faith, and I have actions".* And James counters: *"Show me faith without actions! Instead, I'll show you my faith through my actions"* (2:18). Can you actually say you believe something if there are no visible signs of that belief being demonstrated with tangible actions? Another interesting question might be: Can you actively follow religious rules and rituals with out actually believing? This is not an invitation for us to criticize each other's actions. It is rather, an invitation to examine our own actions for evidence of what we claim to believe. What do my actions demonstrate about my actual belief? Someone once asked, *"If you were on trial for being a Christian, would there be enough evidence to convict you?"*

James' argument gets a bit heated here when he says, *"You believe there is one God. Well, that's good"* (2:19a). This is the basic belief statement of faith for the Hebrew person. There is only one God. This set them apart from all of the other religions of the day. This is what all three of the largest world religions believe today. Christianity, Islam, and Judaism are all *monotheistic*. We all agree that there is only one God. This is because we all trace our faith heritage to that one guy, Abraham. (More about him later). Well, that's good, right? That means we all behave as if we are all following that one God right? We all act as if we are the created, loved, saved, called people of that one God, right? We "believe" there is one God. *"But"* James says, *"Even demons believe that –*

and tremble!" (2:19b). Yikes! Even demons know that there is one
Almighty God. But that "belief" does not change the fact that they
are evil demons! James asks, ***"Want proof, you fool, that faith
without practical action is useless?"*** (2:20). He's getting kind of
touchy about this! It's almost like he is really concerned about the
idea of saying one believes something without actually acting like
it's true. He just called anyone who lives that way a "fool"! So he
offers a couple of examples to convince us:

EXAMPLE ONE: ABRAHAM

James asks, ***"How about old Abraham? Didn't he prove he
believed when he offered up Isaac on the alter?"*** (2:21). If you
need a little refresher, you can find this story in Genesis chapter 22.
God had called Abraham and Sarah out of the land of Ur to be a new
expression of the continuing, expanding relationship He was creating
with humanity. From Genesis 12-21 Sarah and Abraham followed
God through some challenging tests that galvanized their faith in
many ways. But, the greatest challenge happened one morning when
God asked Abraham to literally sacrifice his son, Isaac by burning
him on an alter on top of a mountain. Now, that was weird enough,
but the added challenge was the fact that Isaac was a miracle child, a
gift. Abraham and Sarah were about 100 years old when he was
born! He was their only true child! He was the greatest thing in
their lives! But, God put Abraham to the "test". And Abraham went
through with it. He took Isaac on that three-day journey to that

mountain. He built an alter, made a woodpile, bound Isaac, and placed him on it. But, before he slit his son's throat and burnt him up, God stopped Abraham and said, *"Do not do anything to him. Now I know that you fear God, because you have not withheld from me your son, your only son"* (Gen. 22:12 NIV).

James says, **"See? His faith and his practice worked together. His practice completed his faith. And, the Scripture says, "Abraham actively trusted God, and that counted as faith". And he was called "a friend of God". Can you see that his faith and his practice worked together? Not just through believing alone"** (2:22-24). Now, it's important to point out here that the apostle Paul uses this same example to make a different point. Many people, including Martin Luther might think Paul and James are saying opposite things. Rather, Paul's audience seemed to have a problem with thinking that one's behavior could earn and keep God's love and salvation, while James is making the point that one's love of God, and one's saved state ought to be demonstrated by practical actions. Paul said, *"You foolish Galatians!* (Again, we are reminded of how foolish we are when we get this wrong!) *Who has bewitched you? Before your very eyes Jesus Christ was clearly portrayed as crucified. I would like to learn just one thing from you: Did you receive the Spirit by observing the law, or by believing what you heard? Are you so foolish? After beginning with the Spirit, are you now trying to attain your goal by human effort? Have you suffered so much for nothing — if it really was for nothing? Does God give*

118

you his Spirit and work miracles among you because you observe the law, or because you believe what you heard? Consider Abraham: "He believed God, and it was credited to him as righteousness." Understand, then, that those who believe are children of Abraham. The Scripture foresaw that God would justify the Gentiles by faith, and announced the gospel in advance to Abraham: "All nations will be blessed through you." So those who have faith are blessed along with Abraham, the man of faith" (Galatians 3:1-9 NIV). Paul was denouncing a kind of legalism that was seducing his friends. Legalism is an enemy of the true faith in the finished work of God's actions which makes us, saves us, equips us, and calls us in to active faith-filled love and service. This was especially an issue that Hebrew believers had to grasp, as Gentiles were becoming followers of Christ, but not adherents to Hebrew culture. James is saying that true faith is not a matter of mere intellectual ascent. Rather, we are made, saved, equipped, and called by faith alone, in God alone, but that faith in the "one God" should be demonstrably shown in our actions. Legalism is actions without true faith, while true faith is always demonstrated by faith-filled actions.

EXAMPLE TWO: RAHAB

James' second example is the little story of Rahab found in Joshua chapter 2. He says, **"Likewise, wasn't Rahab the prostitute called faithful because of her actions when she hid those spies and sent them safely off?"** (2:25). This is a sly example for James to bring up after talking about Abraham. Everyone knows that Abraham is the great Father of the three great world religions. He's that upstanding religious guy. But Rahab? She was a pagan prostitute in an enemy town. Just to remind you, the Hebrews had been liberated from slavery in Egypt forty years earlier. After wandering in the wilderness, they finally started to enter 'The Promised Land'. Their first obstacle was the city of Jericho. They sent spies to check it out. Those spies snuck in to Jericho and spent the night at a local brothel. (Now we won't comment on what they were doing there). Anyway, they got to "know" Rahab, and she decided that she was now on their side. And she demonstrated her faith by hiding the spies from the Jericho authorities who were looking for them, and then passing them safely out her exterior wall window. Her help was rewarded when God knocked down Jericho's walls and only her piece of the wall and her family was saved.

Now, Rahab was not "made righteous" by her actions. She was ***"called faithful because of her actions"*** (2:25). She was "seen to be a person of righteous faith". Abraham and Rahab passed the test of actions. Later, Rahab is an even greater example of God utilizing imperfect people (like me) when she becomes an ancestor of King David and ultimately Jesus himself (Matt. 1:5). She put her faith into practice. She even made the author of Hebrew's list of our great ancestors who were commended for *"being sure of what we hope for and certain of what we do not see"* (Hebrews 11:1 NIV) stating, *"By* *faith the prostitute Rahab, because she welcomed the spies, was not killed with those who were disobedient"* (Hebrews 11:31 NIV).

IS IT BREATHING?

James says, **"Like a body without breath is dead, so faith without practical actions is dead"** (2:26). I just read in the news about a woman who was left in a morgue in Carletonville, South Africa in June 2018. Her body was removed from the scene of a fatal car accident. The paramedics saw no evidence of life and delivered her to the morgue. But later, someone at the morgue noticed she that was breathing. Now she is recuperating in the hospital. Is there evidence of Spiritual breath in your life? That's not a judgment. One is not meant to examine another's behavior for signs of Spiritual life. One can examine one's own actions though, to test and see if there is evidence of what one actually believes. Do you actually believe that God uniquely created you, absolutely loves you, sacrificially saved you, has especially equipped and called you in to extraordinary and unique loving service? Do you act like it?

Of course real, breathing, life-giving action is not just any action. It is action in line with the nature of the all-loving God. Abraham Joshua Heschel wrote, *"Unless the outer life expresses the inner world, piety stagnates and intention decays. Man is constantly producing words and deeds, giving them over either to God or to the forces of evil. Every move, every detail, every act, every effort to*

121

match the spiritual and the material, is serious ... Faith knows no boundaries between the will of God and all of life."[33] The "inner" life will be expressed in the "outer" world – whether that expression proves one's inner life is given over to God or to the "forces of evil". In his book, 'Living, Loving, and Learning', Leo Buscaglia tells a story about how, even in our charity we tend to be self-serving. He wrote, "*Recently, in a Midwestern university, there was an interesting sociological experiment with students concerning sharing and giving. They asked that each student bring a dime. They said, "There are people starving in India. There is a plague and they really need help. If you feel that you'd like to give to that, put the dime in an envelope and write on it, "India". That's pretty far away, India. There are some people in a local ghetto, a family, that really need groceries to live now. If you want to help these people, it will be given to them anonymously. Put your dime in an envelope and put "poor family." Now, of course, we don't have a photocopier at the university and we need to get one for those of you who need to copy papers and manuscripts — and make it easily accessible. If you want to help buy a photocopier, put ten cents in the envelope and put "copier"." Eighty percent of that money went to a photocopy machine!*"[34] It's not enough to just check off a list of actions – Was I charitable? Yes! Check! Let's honestly evaluate our

[33] Abraham Heschel, *Man's Quest for God* (London: MacMillan Publishing Co.,1974), 93.
[34] Leo Buscaglia, *Living, Loving & Learning* (Thorofare: Charles B. Slack, Inc., 1982), 149, 150.

own actions and ask, *"Was I really charitable? Was that actually love, or was it really a self-serving action?"*

DO YOU ACTUALLY BELIEVE?

A powerful illustration of putting faith in to action is the story of 'The Great Blondini'.[35] History's most famous tightrope walker was the French acrobat named Jean François Gravelet, better known as Monsieur Charles Blondin. He traveled to America to cross the Niagara Falls on a 1,300 foot, two inch thick hemp rope. On June 30, 1859, about 25,000 people came out to watch him do it. Wearing bright pink tights and carrying a 50 pound, 26 foot long pole, he crossed from the USA to Canada over the falls while a band played "Home, Sweet Home". People were astounded at this feat. But, even more spectacular were his stunts over about 300 more crossings. He strapped a giant daguerreotype camera to his back and stopped half way across, set it up and took a photo of the crowd watching him. He crossed wearing shackles. He crossed at night with only locomotive headlights illuminating the rope at either end. He carried a table and chair on which he sat to eat cake or drink champagne that he acquired from lowering a rope to the passing boat, the 'Maid of the Mist'. He carried people like his manager, Harry Colcord across on his back. His most famous stunt was when

---

[35] G. Linnaeus Banks, *eds., Blondin: His Life and Performances* (London: Routledge, Warne, and Routledge, 1862)

he carried a stove and utensils on his back, stopped half way, lit the stove fire, cooked an omelet which he lowered to the 'Maid of the Mist' to feed her passengers.

On July 15, 1859, US President Millard Fillmore watched Blondini walk across to Canada and come back pushing a wheelbarrow on his rope. Imagine Blondini asking Fillmore, "*Do you believe I can take a man back to Canada in this wheel barrow?*" Fillmore might have said, "Of course I believe that. I just saw you bring it across". Then, 'The Great Blondini' may have said, "*Get in the wheelbarrow*". At that point Fillmore would prove whether he truly believed or not. Was it only a theory, or did he truly believe in Blondini? Christian faith is not a theory. It is a life-style. At our church we started defining "faith" as "risk". If we are not taking risks of trust, in actual, practical demonstrations of belief in a loving, guiding, providing God, can we actually say we believe at all? What might that look like for you?

Let's pray.

> *Dear Lord, by Your Holy Spirit, fill us with the courage we need to act like really believe that You made us, that You really love us, that You have truly saved us, that You have fully equipped us with everything we need to boldly engage in the actions of knowing, loving, and serving You. Amen?*

REFLECT:

How are you doing with your actions?

Have people shown their love for you?

Do you actually believe that God uniquely created you, absolutely loves you, sacrificially saved you, has especially equipped and called you in to extraordinary service?

Do you act like it?

How do you know someone loves you without them proving it through their actions?

When have you gotten in to "the wheelbarrow"?

What risks might God be asking you to take?

EXAMEN:

In quiet attention to God's loving presence, reflect on the challenges of actions.

In gratitude, when have you been strengthened by actions?

How are you feeling about your actions?

What is something about your actions that you can talk to God about?

What is something about your actions you can look forward to?

Seek God's guidance, help, and understanding. Pray about actions.

EXERCISE:

List actions that prove your faith is real

Join a church or community activity that takes you out of your comfort zone

Chapter 7

The Challenge of Words

James 3:1-12

Let's not have many teachers, friends, because teachers will be most strictly judged. We all make mistakes. If anyone didn't make a mistake with their words, they would have already arrived, being in control of their whole life. When you put bits into horse's mouths, you can make them go anywhere you want. How about boats? They can be big, and they can be driven by mighty winds and waves, but with a little rudder pilots can steer them wherever they want. Likewise, tongues are a small part of any person, but they can make gigantic boasts. Think about how a destructive fire is started by a tiny spark. Human speech is a vicious gas leak ready to ignite. It's a source of combustion within us. Sloppy words consume people's whole lives. Corrupt teaching sets people's whole lives on fire. Undisciplined speech spews burning smoke from the rotting local garbage dump. All kinds of animals, birds, reptiles, and sea creatures are being domesticated, and have been

housebroken by people, but no one can perfectly

discipline their own mouth. Human words can be

poisonous, impatiently ready to speak error. With the

same mouth we can speak the good word to, or about

our Lord and Father, and with that same mouth speak

a cutting curse upon other people who are made in

the likeness of God. Out of the same mouth comes

truth and lies, compliments and curses, heaven bound

praise and earth bound complaining. My friends, this

is not right. Does freshwater and salt water flow

from the same source? Do fig trees bear olives or

grapevines bear figs? Likewise, a bitter salt source

cannot produce freshwater.

A FAVORITE TEACHER

Most people can recall a favorite teacher. I fondly remember Miss Mason. She was my grade three teacher. I loved Miss Mason. I was 8 years old and she was probably about 25, but I wanted to marry her. I knew she loved nature. So, one day, when I found a dead bird on the side of the road, I decided to give it to her as a token of my affection. Now, one of the problems with this plan was that I found the dead bird on a Friday, so I had to keep it under wraps for a few days before I could present it to Miss Mason. I took it home, put it in a box, left it on a shelf in my bedroom, and then forgot about it. Some time later, my older brother came into my bedroom and said, *"What is that stink?"* I said, I didn't know. And he went throughout my bedroom, sniffing, following his nose until, of course he found the box. He opened it and it was full of maggots. I said, *"Don't touch that; that's for Miss Mason!"* He said, *"You have to throw this away. It's gross!"* I said, *"No! She'll love it. She loves nature!"* The next day I took it to school and gave it to her. Now, what was so great about Miss Mason was that she was so kind. She said, *"Thank you Jamie! This is beautiful. I'll take it home."* I bet she still has it, and that she still has a very special place in her heart for me.

In Chapter three, James says, ***"Let's not have many teachers, friends, because teachers will be most strictly judged"*** (3:1). You might say, *"Why? What's wrong with teachers? Many of them are*

129

such nice people!" Why would God, through James, say teachers are going to be more harshly judged? What a horrible thing. I mean, that is not a great advertisement for teacher school. Imagine the ads: *"Come and be a teacher! You'll be more harshly judged!"* What is James getting at here? Why are teachers going to be judged more strictly? Well, of course, it's because teaching is dangerous. Words, teaching, and ideas are dangerous things. Teaching is dangerous. You know the saying that *"the pen is mightier than the sword"*. It's true. Words and ideas are powerful. A little a word, a simple idea, can create great control. It can bring great peace, order, and wisdom. Or it can bring utter chaos. It can build up or destroy. Revolutions begin with ideas, a few words, a little teaching.

There are people in prisons today because of what they think and teach. Totalitarian regimes and rulers know that a little idea can bring down a whole government. They know that words, ideas, teachings are stronger than armies. We have seen that in the 20th century. We have seen the most terrible treatment of human beings based on some terrible ideas. We have seen wars start over theories. Teaching is dangerous. We have also seen reconciliation and reconstitution. We have seen the Berlin Wall come down, witnessed official apartheid being dismantled, observed truth and reconciliation being attempted. We have seen new countries start and old ideas die. Teaching is powerful. Auschwitz survivor, writer, and human-rights activist, Elie Wiesel remembers his teenaged conversation with Selishter Rebbe who told him, *"Be careful with words, they're dangerous. Be wary of them. They begat either demons or angels. It's up to you to give life to one or the other. Be careful, I tell you, nothing is as dangerous as giving free rein to words"*.[36]

A REVOLUTIONARY IDEA

Believers in Christ live by a powerful idea, a revolutionary truth; that truth itself is revealed to us by God. It's not based on human opinion or human ideas or things we have been able to work out for ourselves. Truth is something revealed to us by God. In fact, the Word Himself is revealed to us from heaven. We could never have made up the salvation story of God. The gospel message is given to us from God. We could have never figured it out. By God's Word, we know what truth is. And our words (what we say, and teach, and meditate on, and believe) are crucial. We need to work hard to understand what God is revealing to us in his word, and to so very carefully pass this teaching along.

I flew to Toronto this week. As I was strapping in to my seat, the pilot got on the speaker and said, *"Good morning everybody! I just want you all to know that I've never flown a plane before. I've never been to flight school. I've actually never even been in a plane. But I have some really great theories about flight, and airplanes and stuff. So trust me on this. It's going to be a great trip"*. What would you do? Wouldn't you jump off that plane? Why would you trust that

---

[36] Elie Wiesel, *Legends of Our Time* (New York: Schocken Books, 1968), 14.

pilot? Of course that didn't happen. It's a joke. We all assume that when we get on a plane, that person in the uniform has gone to some kind of program somewhere, and has gotten some training and testing and certification to be able to correctly handle that plane. I love when I'm on a plane, and the cockpit door is still open, and I can see the pilot and co-pilot flipping all the switches. I think, *"Oh yeah, she knows what she's doing, look at that!"* But what if she doesn't? What if she's just flipping buttons and switches and guessing at stuff? We make assumptions, don't we? We assume that these people know what they're doing; otherwise they wouldn't give them that uniform? You would never get into a plane with pilots with whom you didn't have absolute confidence in their ability to know where to go and how to get there.

Why would we ever trust somebody with something far more important, the truth of God? Why do we assume, just because something is written down or something is on the Internet, that it's true? Just because somebody says that it's true. Spiritual teaching nurtures our spiritual lives, and I think we need to assume less and be more discerning in what we hear, what we believe, what we read, what we pass on to others. The fact is anybody can write a book. Anybody can get on the radio, anybody can get on TV or on the Internet and start spouting off crazy ideas about God and life and the universe, and we tend to believe them. Why would we? I think James is saying we have got to be careful. Remember, James is concerned about his people. James is back there, in Jerusalem, and he is their pastor, as he's thinking about all the Jewish people who have come to know Christ, but are scattered around the world. Because of persecution, they have gone off to all corners of the Roman world, and he is writing them this letter. He's thinking about these people, and he is deeply concerned that they would believe the Word of God and not all the myths that are going around. And they were going around then just as much as they are going around now. James implores us to make sure that we are very careful in what and how we are teaching; how we are using our words to reflect the essence of God's reality. We have to scrutinize all beliefs, all teachers, and all teaching. Now, we are all teachers because we all teach each other by what we say and what we do. James could as easily say, *"Be careful what you do. Be careful what you say. Because we will all be judged for what we say and do"*.

WE ARE ALL TEACHERS

I don't think he's talking about the final judgment. We are judged whether we believe in Christ or not. That is the judgment for our eternal destiny. But in this life, in this world, people will learn what we think is true based on what we say and do. God teaches us through each other by our actions and by our words. In that sense, we're all teachers, and it's a lovely thing we get to do. We get to teach each other. But we have got to be careful, James is saying. We must strictly judge all teaching. The apostle Peter, Said, *"If anybody speaks (if anybody talks at all, if you talk, or teach) you should do it as one speaking the very words of God"* (1 Peter 4:11 NIV). What else would you want to teach? What else would you want to pass on and teach people, through your words and your actions, other than the truth of God? Why would you want to teach, through your words or actions, anything else?

Remember what James said back in 1:19. He said, *"Be quick to listen (to the word of God) and slow to speak (your own opinions)"*. But, we have to confess, we can be so quick to speak and believe the myths and lies and theories of the world rather than the Word of God. We have got to confess that. We have got to realize that we are creatures who seem to be attuned to keep falling for lies and myths rather than truth. We do. I mean, the things that we pass on to each other, the things that we e-mail to each other, the things that we tell the stories – *"Did you hear about this that happened? Do you know about that?"* And we have nothing to back it up, whether it's true or not. We love to pass something on because it's a great story. And we love to be in these little info bubbles of stuff that just confirms what we already think we already know. It's interesting, isn't it? We can be so slow to listen to or study and believe God's Word, but so quick to pass on myths and lies without doing the research, to find out if it's true. I think we are a lazy culture that doesn't want to spend the time studying; rather we want to pass on myths. It's so much easier. *"Hey, did you hear about this? Hey, did you hear that story? I just got this e-mail. It must be true. It must be true because it came to me by e-mail through the Internet"*. We also need to hold our ideas humbly and with a generosity towards those who may disagree with us.

WE NEED DISCERNMENT

I get things sent to me all the time. People ask me what I think of this book, or that thing on the Internet. I recently watched something on the Internet, and I couldn't believe the crowds that were at this meeting listening to this teacher. The teaching was disturbingly false, but the thing that really disturbed me was the crowd. It's not just that they would show up to hear this guy, but that they would stay. Once the person started spouting their ideas, I was stunned that the people stayed in the room rather than fleeing. They didn't just stay in the room. They clapped. They cheered. They went into ecstatic reverence for what this person was saying. I was stunned. We need much deeper discernment. We must seriously discern all teaching and teachers. We should test every word. Our words are a test of what we actually believe.

Over the years I have constantly been telling people to test any teaching they hear. I tell people to test it to see if it's true. Don't ask if you like an idea. Rather, ask if it's true. One young man really took this challenge to heart. He started challenging me on everything I taught. Everything I said, he'd ask, *"Is that true?"* I would show him where I got my facts from, or how I had parsed a certain Greek verb. He really tested me. I thought it was great.

135

There was one thing I said one time that he really did not believe. It was something about an animal that I was describing, and I said that this indicated the point is in the passage I was teaching on. He said he didn't think what I was saying about that animal was true, and so that teaching on that passage was suspect. He did all this research, and he phoned all over the United States and Canada to some of the leading experts and institutions that know about these animals. Then he came back to me and he said, *"It's not true. Your point was false."* It's funny; I did my little bit of research through the Internet, and I found out that the only places that said that this was true about those animals were only on Christian sites, and that idea showed up early in the 20th century, and only in Christian circles. I was ashamed. I was put in my place, as I should have been. I made a public confession of my mistake and a public commendation of that fine young man who passed the test of words by strictly judging this teacher.

As a teacher, I feel the weight of this. Why would I want to spout something that's not true? I don't want to, but sometimes I do, and I need to be caught out. We ought not to be people who just sit and take any teaching in. We ought to be people who read the bible for ourselves, so that we can smell if something just doesn't seem right. We ought to bring our bibles to church, with pens and note books, to take notes and check things out later. If somebody quotes something from the Bible, look it up to see if it's actually there, if that's what it actually says, or means. I have things in books and thought something didn't make sense. I confronted a popular Christian author one time. He had made some points that I thought were suspect. He had a series of bible references as footnotes for his points. He was basically saying, *"These points are true, look at the bible passages that back me up"*. And he listed the poof text passages. So I looked them all up, and several of them had nothing to do with what he was talking about. Years later, I happened to be at a conference where that guy was speaking. I waited for him after his talk, and, with his book in my hand; I asked him what point he was making by referring to those texts. He said his editor had put them in there. I thought, *"Well, you are a teacher. Didn't you know that you are under greater scrutiny, that you'll be more harshly judged? And I'm doing some of that judging right now!"*

TEST WORDS

We have got to test words. Words are powerful. Sometimes I get in trouble because I love to change the words of songs. I don't want to sing things that aren't true. Sometimes there are popular songs that are just too theologically incorrect. So, sometimes I have changed words in a few songs for our church. What's fun is to go to a conference or to visit another church and see my changes show up in someone else's power point. I'll whisper to the person next to me, *"That's my change. I changed those words"*. Why would you want to sing something that's not true? Words form our lives. Words form our ideas, and ideas form who we are and how we act. Our actions stem out of what we believe. It starts with what we believe and what we put our faith into. Why would we want to believe what's not true and go put it into practice? We believe what we read. We believe what we sing. We believe what we pray. We believe what we preach through our words and our actions to each other, and it's a huge responsibility. In fact, we're all teachers; we're all dangerous; we all should take note.

We need to be vigilant in the testing of words; all that we hear and all that we utter. James says, ***"We all make mistakes. If anyone didn't make a mistake with their words, they would have already arrived, being in control their whole life"*** (3:2). Nobody can completely tame their mouth. We can't be perfect. We stumble in many ways. If anybody was never at fault in what they say (James uses the word "*logos*" which means "word") that one would have already arrived ("be perfect" NIV). He uses the word "*teleios*" there. The word *teleios* means "the end goal". It's the wisdom and maturity that God wants to grow us up in to. No one is perfectly there yet. If you had already arrived at perfect maturity and wisdom, you would be able to keep the whole body in check. That's the challenge of words. Consider if you have complete control over your mouth, your teaching. I know I don't. So I have some growing to do. I get to keep growing in wisdom and maturity.

HORSES, BOATS, TONGUES, FIRE

If we were always perfectly clear in what we hear, believe, and say is true, our whole lives would be true. James uses four metaphors to illustrate this point. He uses a horse, a boat, a tongue, and a fire to show how a little thing -- like a little teaching can be helpful or destructive. The first image he uses is a horse. Even though horses are huge powerful creatures *"when you put bits into horses mouths, you can make them go anywhere you want"* (3:3). You can turn the whole animal with a relatively small thing. Imagine, a huge willful beast, being constrained by a little bit in its mouth, being under control and led wherever you want. While on a camping trip in California with teenagers from Vancouver years ago, we spent a morning horseback riding. My horse seemed extra spunky. I was having a very hard time controlling her. At one point, she took off at a crazy gallop. I was terrified. It got worse as my saddle began to slide sideways. I knew that within a few seconds my saddle would slip completely around and I would be dropped under those pounding hooves. But the young wrangler in charge of our outing galloped up beside me, reached out and firmly took hold of my horse's bridle bit. She slowed and came under control and my life was spared! Of course all my teenaged friends were so entertained by my near death terror. Meanwhile, I learned quickly how to take command of the reigns attached to that little bridle bit and kept my horse well under control from then on.

Secondly, James says, *"How about boats? They can be big, and they can be driven by mighty winds and waves. But, with a little*

rudder pilots can steer them wherever they want" (3:4). No one is as powerful as the winds and waves. But, with a little rudder, one can maneuver a boat against even stormy elements. We have friends who own a medium sized sailboat. One of our favorite things to do is to holiday on their boat with them, sailing around the Salish Sea Gulf Islands. There are times when we have encountered harsh weather and it has amazed me how we can chart a course through even the toughest winds and waves to get where we want to go. The key is the rudder. There are a few dangerous channels that one must navigate through to get where one wants to go in the Gulf Islands. And one must skirt the many ferries, freighters, log booms, and other floating vessels and debris that ply the ocean waters. But, with a steady hand on the wheel, which steers the rudder, one can pilot through even the most dangerous passages.

I had an experience in Mexico years ago that was much more serious. I was there with my in-laws, and I wanted to do some body surfing. Have you ever had this experience? You go out on the water and you are trying to catch that really good wave, and so you go a little further, and a little further. And the next one just looks a little better; so you go a little further, a little further. And suddenly you can't touch the bottom. I was being tossed around, and I turned around. I couldn't believe how far away the beach was. I thought I was within about 20 feet of shore. But I must have been about 200 feet out. And I knew I was about to drown. I had no idea what I was supposed to do, and I was being dragged out. I had no tether. I had no rudder. I was just bobbing in this water, and I knew I would be sucked out to Japan. I just had this one idea. I thought, *"I just have to get my bearings here and swim sideways to the shore"*. I aligned myself diagonally to the shore, and swam and swam and swam sideways, until finally, way down the beach, I found my way out of the rip tide, to some rocks I could climb onto out of the water.

Next, James says, **"Likewise tongues are a small part of any person, but they can make gigantic boasts"** (3:5a). Little tongues can proclaim acts beyond any person's ability. Lies and legends can turn any person into a mythical giant. And, finally James says, **"Think about how a destructive fire is started by a tiny spark"** (3:5b). For the past few summers, Western North America has been experiencing devastating fires. Whole communities have been wiped away in a day. Many times it has been discovered that the cause of the fire was the casual discarding of a used cigarette. A tiny thing, nonchalantly disposed of can destroy land, livelihoods, livestock, and lives.

Loose tongues, like wild horses, windy waves, and scorching fires, are powerful, dangerous things. They can each be harnessed for good, or let loose for absolute destruction. Without a bit or a rudder, you are in trouble. There can be utter chaos. And there is chaos today inside and outside the Church. False teaching is ruining people's lives and whole communities are being destroyed. The apostle Paul, writing to his young protégé, Timothy said, *"The time is going to come when people are not going to put up with sound doctrine. Instead, to suit their own desires, they are going to gather around themselves a great number of teachers who are going to say whatever their itching ears want to hear. They are going to turn their ears away from the truth and turn aside to myths"* (2 Tim. 4:3, 4 NIV). I think James was living in that time. And I think we are still living in that time too. This is the danger that is around us. A little spark, like a little bad teaching, can cause so much damage. Undisciplined, directionless, destructive teaching, like a fire, can burn out of control. But, a little personal discipline and direction can bring all that chaos under control. Good teaching, like a horse or a boat that's under control, can be very useful, very helpful to instruct us, to lead us in the way of knowing, loving, and serving God. Huge things can be accomplished, greater depths of personal transformation can happen. Like a little bit on a horse, like a little rudder on a boat, it can guide us in the right way. A lot can get accomplished. But a fire out of control is devastating. I believe that's James's point here. And I believe that's the choice we have with our mouth, what we say, what we believe, what we teach, through our words. God is inviting us to grow in developing wisdom and maturity in our words.

WISE AND MATURE WORDS

We can grow in having wise and mature words. We can develop a little more bridling, a little more steering to avoid chaos. We can use discernment. I think that's what James is saying here. Like a horse's bit or a ship's rudder, we can learn to wisely control what teaching we listen to, what information we discern, what we choose to believe, and what we carefully teach through word and action. We can pay more attention to God's revealed truth than to the human centered myths and theories and lies that are all around us. And how do we do that? You know how to do that. It's like anything. It's the basics, isn't it? We do that by paying attention to God's loving presence; by remaining in an awareness of His loving embrace, and by meditating on and speaking God's word, nothing less. Otherwise we'll be like an uncontrolled fire. James is serious about this. Remember, the people he is writing to, Jewish Christians, people steeped in the Word of God -- what we call the Old Testament now. They knew it inside and out, as James did. You might know the popular verse Proverbs 29:18. It says, *"Where there is no hazôn (God's revealed truth), the people cast off restraint"*. They'll believe anything. They'll follow anything. They'll go out of control. *"But blessed is the one who keeps (pays attention to the carefully heard, taught, studied, reflected on, obeyed) the Law (the Word of God)"*.

James says, *"Human speech is a vicious gas leak ready to ignite. It's a source of combustion within us. Sloppy words consume people's whole lives. Corrupt teaching sets people's whole lives on fire. Undisciplined speech spews burning smoke from the rotting local garbage dump"* (3:6). Our words can be a *"world of evil among the parts of the body"* (NIV). I think that's true of every individual. It's also true of the body of Christ, the Church. The word *"gehenna"* he uses there ("hell" NIV) was a literal place. "Gehenna" means "the valley of wailing", because before the Tenth Century BC, when Jerusalem became the historic center for the people of God, it was the place where human sacrifices (especially babies) were made to the god Moloch. So it was known as the valley of wailing. That area in Jerusalem later became the main garbage dump of the city by Jesus' and James' day. Jesus used it often as a metaphor for our eternal destiny apart from God. This was the garbage dump he could point to, which was always burning, and always full of maggots; where, *"the worm never sleeps and the fire is never quenched"* (Mark 9:48). I think what James is saying here is that one must test all words. Does your tongue (what you say, what you teach, what you demonstrate that you believe with your actions) come from the garbage dump of humanity, the trash of human distraction and opinion, or from what God reveals to be true?

Henri Nouwen wrote, *"Diadochus of Photiki offers us a very concrete image: "When the door of the steam bath is continually left open, the heat inside rapidly escapes through it; likewise the soul, in its desire to say many things, dissipates its remembrance of God through the door of speech, even though everything it says may be good. Thereafter the intellect, though lacking appropriate ideas, pours out a welter of confused thoughts to anyone it meets, as it no longer has the Holy Spirit to keep its understanding free from fantasy. Ideas of value always shun verbosity, being foreign to confusion and fantasy. Timely silence, then, is precious, for it is nothing less than the mother of the wisest thoughts."* [37]

James reminds us **"all kinds of animals, birds, reptiles, and sea creatures are being domesticated, and have been housebroken by people"** (3:7) **but no one can perfectly discipline their mouth"** (3:8a). So we have got to be careful. We have got to be on our toes. We can't tame our words completely. We have got to be ready and discerning. Because the fact is **"human words can be poisonous, impatiently ready to speak error"** (3:8b). **With the same mouth we can speak the "eulogos" (the good word) to, or about our Lord and Father, and with that same mouth speak the "katara" (the cut down curse) upon other people who are made in the likeness of God** (3:9). **Out of the same mouth comes truth and lies, compliments and curses, heaven bound praise and earth bound complaining."** James says, **"My friends, this is not right"** (3:10). Then he asks some rhetorical questions: **"Does freshwater and salt water flow from the same source?"** If you don't know, it doesn't. **"Friends"**, he says, **"Do fig trees bear olives or grapevines bear figs?"** Again, no they don't. These are rhetorical questions. The answer is no, in case you didn't know that. **"Likewise"**, he says, **"A bitter salt source cannot produce freshwater"** (3:11, 12). We're all

---

[37] Henri Nouwen, *The Way of the Heart* (New York: Ballantine Books, 1981), 37, 38.

teachers and our teaching will either be the living, freshwater of God's word, or it will be the poisoned bitter salt of human myth and opinion. Jesus made the same point in His Sermon on the Mount. He said, *"Watch out for false prophets. They come to you in sheep's clothing, but inwardly they are ferocious wolves. By their fruit you will recognize them. Do people pick grapes from thornbushes, or figs from thistles? Likewise every good tree bears good fruit, but a bad tree bears bad fruit. A good tree cannot bear bad fruit, and a bad tree cannot bear good fruit. Every tree that does not bear good fruit is cut down and thrown into the fire. Thus, by their fruit you will recognize them"* (Matt. 7:15-20 NIV). Likewise, when talking to the Pharisees of his day, Jesus said, *"You brood of vipers, how can you who are evil say anything good? For out of the overflow of the heart the mouth speaks. The good (person) brings good things out of the good stored up in (side), and the evil (person) brings evil things out of the evil stored up in (side). But I tell you that (people) will have to give account on the day of judgment for every careless word they have spoken. For by your words you will be acquitted, and by your words you will be condemned"* (Matt. 12:34-37 NIV).

CHOICE TEACHING

So what are you speaking and listening to? I think you have choices about this, about what you will say and what you will listen to, about who is teaching you, and about who you are teaching and what are you teaching them about. Are you speaking the *eulogos*, the good word, the good word of God's revealed truth, or the *katára,* the calling down curses of human myths and lies? Teachers are going to be more strictly judged because a word of teaching is dangerous. They are going to be more strictly judged because we are so influenced by teachers, and teachers are going to be judged more strictly because we are desperate to hear and know God's Word, God's truth, not lies. Dietrich Bonhoeffer wrote, *"Let your speech be Yea, yea, and Nay, nay." This is not to say that the disciples are no longer answerable to the omniscient God for every word they utter, it means that every word they utter is spoken in his presence, and not only those words which are accompanied by an oath. Hence they are forbidden to swear at all. Since they always speak the whole truth and nothing but the truth, there is no need for an oath, which would only throw doubt on the veracity of all their other statements. That is why the oath is "of the evil one." But a disciple must be a light even in his words".*[38]

So we need to take this very seriously, and the best cure for myths and lies, the junk food of crummy teaching, is the good steady diet of biblical truth. It's not always popular. God's speech will usually be contra-diction. Contrary speech. It will contradict what we believe naturally. It's not necessarily comfortable words. A teacher's job is to comfort the afflicted and afflict the comfortable. And you are a teacher in what you say and what you do, and your job is to demand nothing but the word of God to be taught in our

---

[38] Dietrich Bonhoeffer, *Life Together*, (New York: Harper & Row, 1954), 37, 38.

churches, in our home groups, in our relationships, and what comes out of your mouth. What you believe is what's going to come out of your mouth and what's going to dictate your actions. Let it be the living *eulogos*, the good word in our neighborhoods today. God is inviting you to grow in His control over your teaching.

Let's pray.

Dear God, we thank you that you didn't leave us in the dark to try to figure You out. You have come. You have revealed yourself in what You have said and what's been recorded in the word, the scriptures. We thank You that You came, the good Word, who took on flesh and walked for a while amongst us. Lord, we thank You that You have put us in the very places we are and that today we get to proclaim the good news. God, use this moment, that you would teach us and that we would teach others Your truth. Help us to listen to You today. Help us let You have full control over our words. Amen?

REFLECT:

Who are the trustworthy teachers you know?

What are you listening to?

What does your speech say about you?

What "good words" are you giving your neighbors?

When have you words gotten you in to trouble?

When have you experienced the spark of bad words causing a fire?

EXAMEN:

In quiet attention to God's loving presence,

reflect on the challenge of words.

In gratitude, when have you been strengthened by words?

How are you feeling about words?

What is something about words that you can talk to God about?

What is something about words you can look forward to?

Seek God's guidance, help, and understanding.

Pray about your words.

EXERCISE:

Bring your bible, a notebook and a pen to church.

Make notes on the sermon.

Intentionally say good words to the important people in your life.

Make note of the effects of good words said to people.

Chapter 8

The Challenge of Wisdom

James 3:13-18

Who is wise and understanding among you? Let them show it by living well and doing good work with gentleness that comes from true wisdom. But, if you have bitterness and strife in your heart, don't be boasting and lying. That kind of false wisdom is not from above, but rather from below, and is merely worldly human opinion and demonic lies. For wherever there is bitterness and strife, there's confusion and every kind of evil practice. But, the wisdom that comes from above is firstly pure, then peaceful, gentle, rational, full of mercy and good results, impartial and sincere. The results of this kind of right living is flourishing peace.

James' next invitation to an opportunity to grow in faith that James addresses is the challenge of wisdom. He says, ***"Who is wise and understanding among you? Let them show it by living well and doing good work with gentleness that comes with true wisdom"*** (3:13). James is saying that he is not impressed with anyone claiming to be "wise". He is not interested in anyone's status or intellectual knowledge. He is interested in how one puts that knowledge into real life practice. It's not enough to have the right knowledge. One must have "right use" of that knowledge. The great English Baptist preacher, Charles Spurgeon said, *"Wisdom, I suppose, is the right use of knowledge. To know is not to be wise. Many men know a great deal, and are all the greater fools for it. There is no fool so great a fool as a knowing fool. But to know how to use knowledge is to have wisdom".*[39] Both James and Spurgeon call those who have knowledge without "right use" of that knowledge, "fools". God is inviting all of us to grow in the wisdom of living well.

I was with a group of students who were visiting with the London Anglican preacher, Dick Lucas one time. He told us a story about when he was invited to speak at an English boy's school during their traditional weekly chapel. This would be a routine, ceremonial thing for that school, and every boy, as well as the whole staff would be in

---

[39] Charles Spurgeon's Sermon, *The Fourfold Treasure* (1871).

obligatory attendance. Dick took the opportunity to proclaim the basic Gospel message, even inviting people to respond to God's free gift of life in Christ, by faith. Later, during the post service tea in the faculty lounge, the Head master of the school politely addressed Dick saying, "*I used to believe all that, about God and so on. But, of course, when I became educated, I gave all that up*". Dick looked at him and calmly said, "*Well then you're a fool*". The Head Master nearly spilt his tea sputtering, "*What!!??*" Dick said, "*The bible says, the fool says in his heart, "There is no God*" (Psalm 14:1). *So you are a fool*". The biblical idea of wisdom is the skill to live rightly. This living "rightly" is what the bible calls "righteousness". It is living in right relationship with God. The basic skills of doing that, is what "wisdom" is. It is not extra knowledge, but the right use of knowledge.

BITTERNESS AND STRIFE

"*The fear of the LORD is the beginning of wisdom*" (Proverbs 9:10). But it is only the beginning. Wisdom is something that must be developed, over time, in real life application. It takes a lifetime to develop the life skills to live life well. The Hebrew word for "fool" in Proverbs 9:10 is "*naval*". It denotes someone, not with a lack of intellectual prowess, but one lacking moral character. The test of whether one is wise is not about how much one knows, but how one lives. So, James means that the proof of true wisdom is "*living well*", "*doing good work*", and "*gentleness*". Then he ads, **"But, if** *you have bitterness and strife in your heart, don't be boasting and lying"* (3:14). Many people think that they are "wise". But true wisdom is seen in how one lives. And, how one lives proves one to be either wise, or a boasting liar. The test of wisdom is a moral one. It really doesn't matter how much one knows. Are you *"living well", "doing good work",* and being *"gentle",* or is your life full of *"bitterness and strife"?* Any so-called wisdom that comes from a heart of *"bitterness and strife"* usually leaves a trail of bitterness and strife in its wake. True wisdom will always be humble and beneficial to others. Commenting on the kind of so-called wisdom that leaves others bitter and strife filled, James says, *"That kind of false wisdom is not from above, but rather from below, and is merely worldly human opinion and demonic"* (3:15). The source of true wisdom is God. The sources of false wisdom are human opinions and the Devil.

The words James uses that I have translated as "human opinion" ("earthly, unspiritual" NIV) are *"epigeio"* and *"psucho". Epigeio* is the stuff of this world. It is not necessarily evil. It is simply stuck in this plane. It has only this perspective, rather than the perspective of God. We can only know what we can perceive from the experience of our five senses. We can know a lot through the study of the stuff of this world through science and history. But, that is very limited. The apostle Paul says, *"Now we see but a poor reflection as in a mirror"* (1 Cor. 13:12 NIV). We cannot depend only on our five senses to reliably tell us anything of the Spiritual realm. We can only truly know things of the Spiritual realm by faith in the revelations of one from that realm. Christians believe God has spoken, acted, and visited from that other realm. He has revealed everything we need to know for life and faith; not everything there is to know, or everything we want to know, but everything we need to know. But we have to receive it and believe it by faith. Otherwise we are stuck with only an earthly perspective. And that will only give us an earthly wisdom. It will answer some of the vital life questions we have about when and how, but none of the questions about why and who. God's Word (creation, Scripture, Jesus) articulate together God's revelation.

The word psucho is where we get our word for psychology. Again, this is not something necessarily evil. It is simply stuff we think. Our minds are amazing instruments for organizing the input from our five senses. But, again, they are limited instruments, and limited thinking can devolve into psychosis. Depending on the input we receive, one's mind can be tricked. Whether it is false information, or damaging chemicals, one's mind can be altered to cause one to experience and believe all kinds of foolishness leading to bitterness and strife.

But James also suggests another source of the bitterness and strife that we experience. It is the demonic forces of the Spiritual realm. Christians believe that God is not the only source of impact from the Spiritual realm. There are evil forces at play, led by the deceiving tempter himself, the Devil. By faith Christians trust the revelation of God in Jesus and the Scriptures to guide us in knowing what is ultimately true and false. Our own senses may fool us. The demonic forces certainly want to fool us. True Spiritual wisdom comes from (correctly) receiving and believing the revelation of God through His Word written (the bible) and revealed in Jesus (the Word in the flesh), and experienced (in His creation). We also have God, the Spirit living in us, "guiding us into all truth" (John 16:13). So, what are you putting your trust in: your own, or someone else's human opinion, or the Devil, or God's revealed truth? James warns us that looking for wisdom from anything other than God's revealed truth will only lead to confusion and wickedness. He says, *"For wherever there is bitterness and strife, there's confusion and every kind of evil practice"* (3:16).

EXUDING GOOD WILL

In contrast to the bitterness, strife, and confusion of human opinions and demonic influence, James describes the results of God's wisdom: *"But, the wisdom that comes from above is firstly pure, then peaceful, gentle, rational, full of mercy and good results, impartial and sincere"* (3:17). This is similar to Paul's description of the fruit of the Spirit: *"love, joy, peace, patience, kindness, goodness, faithfulness, gentleness and self-control"* (Galatians 5:22, 23 NIV). True wisdom will always exude goodwill. Here's another test of true wisdom, another way you can tell if something or someone is wise: Wisdom will always be pure, peaceful, gentle, rational, merciful, good, impartial, and sincere. This is what wise living looks like.

James says, ***"The results of this kind of right living makes peace flourish"*** (3:18). I believe he is again quoting from Jesus' 'Sermon on the Mount' when the Lord said, *"Blessed are the poor in spirit ... those who mourn ... the meek ... those who hunger and thirst for righteousness ... the merciful ... the pure in heart ... the peacemakers"* (Matthew 5:3-9 NIV). These are the kinds of characteristics of true wisdom. And these characteristics will "make peace flourish". The authentic work of God through His servants will spread God's peace in the world. Ultimately there will be greater peace and redemption as God does His work of *"reconciling the world to himself in Christ, not counting men's sins against them. And he has committed to us the message of reconciliation"* (2 Cor. 5:19 NIV). We have the commission from God to share the ***"gentleness that comes with true wisdom"*** (3:13) in the world. This is God's message of His peace to the world.

Now, when I hear the word "peace", I usually think of the hippies from my childhood in the late 1960's. One Sunday, in 1969, after church, my Father drove our family to a local park. We walked to the top of a small hill and looked down over the park, which was filled with a gathering of "flower children". My father said, *"Kids, those are hippies. Never become one"*. Then we drove home for lunch. What do you think of when you hear the word "peace"? What does the kind of "peace" that God wants to "flourish" look like? Remember Jesus said, *"Peace I leave with you; my peace I give you. I do not give to you as the world gives. Do not let your hearts be troubled and do not be afraid"* (John 14:27 NIV). The "peace" God wants to flourish is "not" like what the world offers. How does the world try to "give" peace?

A SERENITY GARDEN?

I can think of three ways the world tries to "give" peace. The first is a kind of quiet serenity garden. It's an environment of tranquility; a physical space where noise and bother have been eliminated. Some might even equate that with a feeling of "spirituality". But this is not reality. It is not real life. It is certainly not real Christian Spirituality. True Christian Spirituality is about real (messy) life. The motto of the Apollo 11 flight was *"We come in peace for all mankind."* This motto was on the plaque, which was deposited on the face of the moon. [40] The landing was on the "Sea of Tranquility". Armstrong and Aldrin found a tranquil and peaceful scene on the moon. That's because there had never been any humans there to disturb the peace. Apparently, the Roman Emperor, Augustus heard that a certain man living in Rome slept quietly and took his ease every night despite having a great burden of debt. So

---

[40] "Lunar Plaque." Wikipedia. Last modified December 28, 2018, https://en.wikipedia.org/wiki/Lunar_plaque.

Augustus bought the bed that the man slept in. Needless to say, it was a useless purchase for the great Emperor.

Christian peace is not the escape of chaos into the bliss of unhuman, temporary tranquility. Rather, it is the confidence in God's truth no matter what the circumstances. I heard a story of two artists who set out to make pictures representing perfect peace. The first painted a scene depicting a carefree boy sitting in a boat on a little placid lake without a ripple to disturb the surface. The other artist painted a raging waterfall with winds whipping the spray about. On a limb, over hanging the swirling water, a bird had built its nest, and sat peacefully brooding upon her eggs. Here she was safe from her predatory enemies shielded and protected by the roaring falls. Real "peace" is confidence in the midst of chaos. The opposite of peace is not war but fear. Real peace is lack of anxiety. I was attending a conference one time during a very difficult period in my life. I was worried about many things. During a staff meeting at the conference, a group of us were at a meeting with the speaker, Juan Carlos Ortiz. I was hardly paying attention as other staff asked Ortiz some questions. One person asked him, *"What is the greatest challenge facing Christian leaders today?"* Ortiz looked right at me and decisively said, *"Worry!"* I was stunned. He didn't know me, or anything about my personal circumstances. I was a stranger sitting on the floor in a crowded room of conference staff. But he pegged me! I was fraught with worry. I was distracted from anything God wanted to say or do in or through me. The apostle Paul wrote, *"Do not be anxious about anything, but in everything, by prayer and petition, with thanksgiving, present your requests to God. And the peace of God, which transcends all understanding, will guard your hearts and your minds in Christ Jesus. Finally, brothers, whatever is true, whatever is noble, whatever is right, whatever is pure, whatever is lovely, whatever is admirable — if anything is excellent or praiseworthy — think about such things. Whatever you have learned or received or heard from me, or seen in me — put it into practice. And the God of peace will be with you"* (Phil. 4:6-9 NIV). Real peace is trust in Jesus. Trust comes from faith in God, which looks like trust for today and hope for tomorrow. It comes from thinking about whatever is "true, noble, right, pure, lovely, admirable, excellent or praiseworthy". That sums up Jesus! We can rest in God's loving arms and enjoy the faithful presence of Jesus. God invites us to set our minds on the true, noble, right, pure, lovely, admirable, and excellent Lord Jesus who is beside you right now. His Spirit is in you, welcoming you into the comforting presence of God's Holy Community (Father, Son, and Holy Spirit). They surround you with love right now. It also involves "putting into practice whatever we have learned or received or heard from (Paul)". That means applying all the promises of God to your everyday life and living as if it's all true. That's how "the God of peace will be with you".

THE ELIMINATION OF CONFLICT?

A second way the world tries to "give" peace is through trying to eliminate conflict. Is real peace simply a lack of conflict? Is real peace just pacification? Is it simply an absence of war? Is that what God meant when the angels promised, *"Glory to God in the highest heaven, and on earth peace among those whom he favors"* (Luke 2:14 NIV)? If that's what God was promising, it's been a long time coming. Or did He fail at it. Because there has never been an end to human conflict and war. There are bombs going off somewhere in the world every day. I read somewhere that apparently only about eight percent of the time over the last 3,000 years has the world been entirely at peace. In over 3,200 years, only 286 years have been warless and 8,000 treaties have been broken in that time. We don't want war. Surely God doesn't want war. But if the point of God's promised peace is an end to wars, why is there so much personal and global conflict? And doesn't God even command warfare in the Old Testament? Can we actually stop wars?

I read somewhere about Patrice Tamao of the Dominican Republic, who on January 30, 1973 apparently allowed himself to be nailed to a cross *"as a sacrifice for world peace and understanding among men"*. As thousands watched on television, six-inch stainless steel nails were driven through his hands and feet. Tamao had planned to remain on the cross for 48 hours, but after only 20 hours he had to cut short his voluntary crucifixion because of an infection in his right foot. The newspaper article had as it's heading, *"Crucifixion-for-peace falls short"*.

We often talk about "keeping the peace". But do we merely mean inertia? Is some "peace keeping" going along with the world? Is it sometimes just not wanting to rock the boat, or not bringing up embarrassing truth? We tend to want life to be nice and placid. We want nice and placid words from God. Then Jesus says something nasty like "*sell everything and give to the poor.*" (Mark 10:21). In fact, at another point, Jesus said, "*Do you think that I have come to bring peace to the earth? No, I tell you, but rather division!*" (Luke 12:51 NIV). He said, "*Whoever acknowledges me before men, I will also acknowledge him before my Father in heaven. But whoever disowns me before men, I will disown him before my Father in heaven. "Do not suppose that I have come to bring peace to the earth. I did not come to bring peace, but a sword. For I have come to turn "'a man against his father, a daughter against her mother, a daughter-in-law against her mother-in-law — a man's enemies will be the members of his own household.' "Anyone who loves his father or mother more than me is not worthy of me; anyone who loves his son or daughter more than me is not worthy of me; and anyone who does not take his cross and follow me is not worthy of me*" (Matt. 10:32-38 NIV). That's not nice and placid! Christian peace is not rest from conflict. We are at war with sin and death and the Devil.

Christian Spirituality is not an escape from conflict. In fact, it is an invitation to a deeper conflict. We are called to engage in a deeper wrestling match with God. The Old Testament patriarch, Jacob wrestled all night with God (spoiler: God won the fight). In the morning, God changed Jacob's name to "Israel". The name means, "One who wrestles with God". That's who each of us is when we enter this relationship with God. It is a natural conflict between two naturally warring beings (God and humanity). In his article "And Reach As You Go", Floyd Doud Shafer says, in part, the job of a church congregation is to *"Throw (a Christian leader) into the ring to box with God until he learns how short his arms are. Engage him to wrestle with God all the night through. And let him come out only when he is bruised and beaten into being a blessing".*[41] True Christian spirituality is not an avoidance of conflict. It is an invitation to a deeper conflict; to engage more deeply with God; to engage in the wrestling match of personal spiritual transformation; to wrestle with sin and the Devil.

Some have compared our spiritual struggle with that of the Allies at the end of World War Two. Though the war was decisively over after the Allies had conclusively landed in Europe, there were months of warfare to beat the conquered enemy back to their final defeat. Likewise, Satan, sin, and death have been decisively beaten by the life, death, resurrection, and ascension of Jesus Christ. But, there has so far been two thousand years of conflict in a victory march, beating the conquered enemies back to their final defeat.

---

[41] Floyd Doud Shafer, "And Reach As You Go", Christianity Today, March 27, 1961.

God's real peace is "shalom". That word means "wholeness", or "well being". It is not a lack of war, but a conflicted world, conquered by God's war of love, with everything submitted to Him, and freed by Him into active service in this continuing victory march. In His 'Sermon on the Mount' Jesus said, *"Blessed are the peacemakers"* (Matthew 5:9 NIV). But He also said, *"Blessed are those who are persecuted because of righteousness ... Blessed are you when people insult you, persecute you and falsely say all kinds of evil against you because of me. Rejoice and be glad, because great is your reward in heaven, for in the same way they persecuted the prophets who were before you. You are the salt of the earth"* (Matthew 5:10-13 NIV).

A PEACEFUL EASY FEELING?

In 1972, The Eagles sang, *"I got a peaceful, easy feeling"*. Is that a description of true Christian Spirituality? Is it essentially a feeling that we have because we are in relationship with the Living God? Sometimes people say, *"I've got a peace about that decision"*, or *"God hasn't given me a peace about that."* Though our feelings are real, and can alert us to real joy and pain, can they really ever tell us what's true or right? Do people have a peaceful feeling going to martyrdom? Some people have a peaceful feeling about sinning! True Christian peace is not a sentimental feeling. Real Christian peace is active conduct. Peace, like love, is not a feeling but a verb – an action. Jesus said: *"Blessed are the peacemakers for they will be* called *sons of God"* (Matt. 5:9 NIV). It is action, not inaction. We must wage peace! Waging peace is about believing and receiving God's peace and actively passing it on to others. Peace has to start with our relationship with God. Then it will change our conduct from the inside out. Then it will change all your relationships: family & friends, neighborhoods and work places, our cities, countries, and the world.

How does Jesus give peace? Not as the world does. The world tries to have peace through fear, inertia, or mere feelings. Jesus gives us confidence instead of fear. He gives us struggle instead of inertia. He calls us into active conduct instead of sentimental feelings. I believe this is what Jesus was meaning when He said, *"You are the salt of the earth. But if the salt loses its saltiness, how can it be made salty again? It is no longer good for anything, except to be thrown out and trampled by men. You are the light of the world. A city on a hill cannot be hidden. Neither do people light a lamp and put it under a bowl. Instead they put it on its stand, and it gives light to everyone in the house. In the same way, let your light shine before men, that they may see your good deeds and praise your Father in heaven"* (Matt. 5:13-16 NIV). Through Jesus, God has purchased the peace treaty with His rebellious creation. It is a peace treaty between warring enemy factions: God vs. His rebellious creatures. It cost the sacrifice of Jesus Christ. It must be surrendered to on God's terms. It must be engaged in active service to God.

TRUE PEACE

There is an old hymn that was written by Horatio Gates Spafford after two major traumas in his life. The first was the great Chicago Fire of October 1871, which ruined him financially. (He had been a wealthy businessman). Shortly after, while crossing the Atlantic, all four of Spafford's daughters died in a collision with another ship. Spafford's wife Anna survived and sent him the now famous, two-word telegram, *"Saved alone."* Several weeks later, as Spafford's own ship passed near the spot where his daughters had died, the Holy Spirit inspired him to write the words to his famous hymn. These words speak to the eternal confidence that all believers have, no matter what life brings.

> *When peace, like a river, attendeth my way,*
> *When sorrows like sea billows roll;*
> *Whatever my lot, Thou has taught me to say,*
> *It is well, it is well, with my soul.*

> *Tho' Satan should buffet, tho' trials should come,*
> *Let this blest assurance control,*
> *That Christ has regarded my helpless estate,*
> *And hath shed His own blood for my soul.*

That's peace! ***"The wisdom that comes from above is firstly pure, then peaceful, gentle, rational, full of mercy and good results and*** *sincerity.* **The results of this kind of right living makes peace flourish"** (3:17, 18).

Let's pray.

> *Oh Lord, guide us into all wisdom – for Your sake. Give us the powerful realization of the peace we have with You because of Jesus Christ. We confess that we have lived in bitterness and strife. But we give You our whole lives anew, to serve You in purity, peace, gentleness, reason, mercy, goodness, impartiality, and sincerity. Let Your peace flourish in us, in our lives and in our neighborhoods. Amen?*

REFLECT:

When have you encountered true wisdom?

When have you experienced bitterness?

When have you experienced strife?

Have you made peace with God?

In what circumstances is it hardest for you to be "wise"?

EXAMEN:

In quiet attention to God's loving presence, reflect on the challenges
of wisdom.

In gratitude, when have you been strengthened by wisdom?

How are you feeling about wisdom?

What is something about wisdom that you can talk to God about?

What is something about wisdom you can look forward to?

Seek God's guidance, help, and understanding. Pray for wisdom.

EXERCISE:

Consider the eight characteristics of wisdom (James 3:17):

| Purity | Peace | Gentleness | Reason |
| Mercy | Goodness | Impartiality | Sincerity |

Think of an issue in your life where there is bitterness and strife.

Imagine Jesus counteracting this issue with each of these
characteristics of wisdom.

What differences does "wisdom" bring to that issue? Repeat!

Chapter 9

The Challenge of Desires

James 4:1-12

Where do fights and strife come from? Don't they come from conflicting desires that battle within you? You desire what you don't have, so you kill. You're jealous because you don't have what you want. You argue and fight and don't get your own way because you don't ask. You demand but you're not satisfied because you look to the wrong things to give you fulfillment. Don't you know that this is adultery? That's because you are loving the world rather than God. This makes God your enemy. Any one who lives to serve pleasure becomes an enemy of God. Or do you think that Scripture is wrong when it says God is jealous for the Spirit whom He placed in us? But God gives us even more free gifts. God says, "I resist the arrogant, but show favor to the humble". Surrender to God. And, like God, resist the arrogant enemy and it will leave you. Draw near to God and He will be near to you. Wash your wayward hands. Centre your wayward hearts. Grieve and mourn and weep. Turn crying into laughing and joy into mourning. Humble yourselves before the Lord and He will lift you up. Friends, don't slander each other. For the one who condemns a brother or sister judgmentally, misuses the law. And when you misuse the law, you make yourself the lawmaker and judge. There is only one Law Maker and Judge. He is the only one who can save or destroy. Who do you think you are to judge your neighbor?

CONFLICTING DESIRES

James introduces the next opportunity to grow in faith by asking, *"Where do fights and strife come from"* (4:1a). He has just finished talking about what true Christian peace is. Then he turns to address the question of where all of our conflict originates. He sates, *"Don't they come from conflicting desires that battle within you? You desire what you don't have, so you kill. You're jealous because you don't have what you want. You argue and fight and don't get your own way because you don't ask"* (4:1b, 2). We have battling desires inside us. We were designed and created to be creatures that perfectly love God. But we have been deceived and turned inside out looking for other things to satisfy us. Someone said, *"It's like I have two dogs fighting inside me; a good dog and a bad dog."* And when you ask him, *"Which dog wins?"* he says, *"The one I feed."* In his Sermon on the Mount Jesus said, *"No one can serve two masters. Either he will hate the one and love the other, or he will be devoted to the one and despise the other. You cannot serve both God and money"* (Matt. 6:24 NIV). Likewise, the apostle John wrote, *"Do not love the world or anything in the world. If anyone loves the world, the love of the Father is not in him. For everything in the world — the cravings of sinful man, the lust of his eyes and the boasting of what he has and does — comes not from the Father but from the world"* (1 John 2:15, 16 NIV). There are two competing desires in every human heart; two masters. It's either desire of God (the heart set on knowing, loving, and serving God), or desire of the world (the cravings of our sin, the lust of our eyes, and the boasting of what we have and do). These are two dogs fighting. So, which dog are you feeding? The challenge is not whether there are two dogs fighting in your soul. It is which desire you are feeding. One is "living by the flesh". The other is "living by the Spirit". The apostle Paul wrote, *"So I say, live by the Spirit, and you will not gratify the desires of the sinful nature. For the sinful nature desires what is contrary to the Spirit, and the Spirit what is contrary to the sinful nature. They are in conflict with each other, so that you do not do what you want"* (Gal. 5:16, 17). Desire itself is not bad. The problem is in a desire's source. Jeff Imbach wrote, *"Desire is not wrong. But desire that is disconnected from its source in God's desire—and therefore, focused on our own ways of finding life outside of God—is life destroying"*.[42]

ASKING, SEEKING, KNOCKING

James says, **"You argue and fight and don't get your own way because you don't ask"** (4:2). Again, I think he is quoting Jesus' Sermon on the Mount. Matthew 5 - 7 is one long chat. Jesus was explaining about "The Kingdom of God". His point can be summed up: *"I'm the King - You are not"*. Near the end of that sermon, Jesus said, *"Ask and it will be given to you; seek and you will find; knock and the door will be opened to you. For everyone who asks receives; he who seeks finds; and to him who knocks, the door will*

---

[42] Jeff Imbach, *The River Within* (Abbotsford: Fresh Wind Press, 2007), 108.

be opened. Which of you, if his son asks for bread, will give him a stone? Or if he asks for a fish, will give him a snake? If you, then, though you are evil, know how to give good gifts to your children, how much more will your Father in heaven give good gifts to those who ask him!" (Matt. 7:7-11 NIV). We are feeding the wrong dog in the battle for the very soul of our desires when we are not "asking" God.

God's Kingdom is a gift. It is something we receive. The word Jesus uses in Matthew 7:7 for "given" is *dothesetai*. It is a future passive verb. This is something that is simply received. We can't earn it. We have no right to it. It is simply received by those who "ask". Likewise, the "finding" (*euresete*) and the doors being "opened" (*anoigestai*) are gifts. The receiving, finding, and opening of doors that Jesus is talking about are all passively acquired things. They are free gifts. Too often, instead of asking, seeking, and knocking, we are demanding, inventing, and barging. We think we have to produce it. I find it so hard to actually receive a gift. I want to deserve it. Even at Christmas time, we don't actually give and receive free gifts. We barter with them. Think about those for whom you buy gifts. Isn't it only those from whom you receive gifts? Have you ever received a gift from someone you didn't buy one for? Didn't you feel terrible about it? Or have you ever bought something for someone, and them felt a little bad that they didn't get you something? Isn't it because we can't really give and receive free gifts? I want to feel like I have earned it, or deserved it. So, instead

172

of humbly asking, seeking, and knocking, I demand my rights, invent my just desserts, and barge in to take what I desire. James says, **"You demand but you're not satisfied because you look to the wrong things to give you pleasurable fulfillment"** (4:3).

We look to the things of this world to fulfill us. In reality, all desires are actually a search for our true desire, which is God. In the novel, *The World, the Flesh and Father Smith*, the title character has a conversation with a provocative young woman who is the consummate modern atheist. She accuses the priest's religion of being *"only a substitute for sex"*. Father Smith replies, *"I still prefer to believe that sex is a substitute for religion and that the young man who rings the bell at the brothel is unconsciously looking for God"*.[43] Likewise, John Powell wrote, *"There is in each of us a dynamic, a mystique or drive that, unless detoured by human selfishness, leads to search for God, whether we know it or not. It is this desire that carries us beyond what we can see into the darkness and obscurity of faith. It is a hunger that can be satisfied in God alone. Obviously, God does not intend to satisfy this desire completely in this world; its function is to draw us closer and closer to God who alone can give us complete satisfaction. This is the truth which St. Augustine discovered, after the discouragement of so many blind alleys: "our hearts were made for you, 0 God, and they shall not rest until they rest in you"."* [44] Julian of Norwich wrote, *"We will find no rest in*

---

[43] Bruce Marshall, *The World, the Flesh and Father Smith*, (Boston: Houghton Mifflin Co., 1945).

[44] John Powell, *A Reason to Live, A Reason to Die*, (Nilkes: Argus

our heart or spirit as long as we seek it in insignificant things which cannot satisfy us, rather than God".[45]

Though we naturally rebel against our created purpose of glorifying God, when we turn our hearts toward God (feed the good dog), God actually gives us the true desires of our hearts. The psalmists wrote, *"Praise the LORD, O my soul; all my inmost being, praise his holy name. Praise the LORD, O my soul, and forget not all his benefits — who forgives all your sins and heals all your diseases, who redeems your life from the pit and crowns you with love and compassion, who satisfies your desires with good things so that your youth is renewed like the eagle's"* (Psalm 103:1-5 NIV), and *"You open your hand and satisfy the desires of every living thing. The LORD is righteous in all his ways and loving toward all he has made. The LORD is near to all who call on him, to all who call on him in truth. He fulfills the desires of those who fear him; he hears their cry and saves them"* (Psalm 145:16-19 NIV), and *"Do not fret because of evil men or be envious of those who do wrong; for like the grass they will soon wither, like green plants they will soon die away. Trust in the LORD and do good; dwell in the land and enjoy safe pasture. Delight yourself in the LORD and he will give you the desires of your heart* (Psalm 37:1-4 NIV).

Communications, 1975), 106.
[45] Julian of Norwich, *All Will Be Well* (Notre Dame: Ava Maria Press, 1995), 16.

In fact, as we let Him, God can take control of our desires and transform them towards His desires. Hannah Whitall Smith wrote, *"God's promise is, that He will work in us to will as well as to do of His good pleasure. This of course means that He will take possession of our will and work it for us, and that His suggestions will come to us, not so much commands from the outside, as desires springing up within. They will originate in our will; we shall feel as though we wanted to do so and so, not as though we must. And this makes it a service of perfect liberty; for it is always easy to do what we desire to do, let the accompanying circumstances be as difficult as they may . . . The way in which the Holy Spirit, therefore, usually works in this direct guidance is to impress upon the mind a wish or desire to do or to leave undone certain things."* [46]

James says that we demand to have our wayward desires satisfied, and they are not truly satisfying, because we are looking to the wrong things to satisfy our wrong desires (4:3). He ads, **"Don't you know that this is adultery? Because you are loving the world rather than God. This makes God your enemy. Any one who lives to serve pleasure becomes an enemy of God"** (4:4). James calls loving the world ahead of God "adultery"! Marital faithfulness and sexual intimacy are common metaphors in the bible for our relationship with God. Like a married person, if one turns one's desires towards someone other than one's spouse, that is adultery –

---

[46] Hannah Whitall Smith, *The Christian's Secret of a Happy Life*, (New Jersey: Spire Books, Fleming H. Revell Co., 1942), 71, 72.

especially if it is acted upon in sexual intimacy. So it is with God. Our desires are either turned toward God, our not. And God is a jealous God.

A JEALOUS GOD

James asks, *"Or do you think that Scripture is wrong when it says God is jealous for the Spirit whom He placed in us?"* (4:5). What does that mean? Well, James is referring to Old Testament passages like Exodus 20:3, 5: *"You shall have no other gods before me ... You shall not bow down to them or worship them; for I, the LORD your God, am a jealous God"*, Exodus 34:14: Ex. 34:10, 14: *"Then the LORD said: "I am making a covenant with you (like a marriage vow) ... Do not worship any other god, for the LORD, whose name is Jealous, is a jealous God"*, and Deuteronomy 4:23, 24: *"Be careful not to forget the covenant (vows) of the LORD your God that he made with you; do not make for yourselves an idol in the form of anything the LORD your God has forbidden. For the LORD your God is a consuming fire, a jealous God"*. Like a spouse, God wants the undivided love of our hearts completely devoted to Him. So when we pursue other "loves" (wordly desires) God is "jealous". What is God jealous of? God is jealous of our devotion and intimacy.

Several times, early in my courtship of Liz, while we were living in separate cities, I wanted to get to her so badly I drove all night across our province. One time, several of us university students were gathering at Liz's hometown to work as tree planters that summer. There were other boys whom I knew she liked, and whom I knew her parents would naturally be more impressed with than with me. I wanted to be the first one to arrive in her town and at her parent's home for that vital first impression. So, I convinced a few friends to make the trip a few days earlier than all the others. I was jealous for Liz's attention and for the attention of her family. But, the group I was traveling with had car trouble. We were delayed for several days. With each passing hour, I was tormented with frustrating jealousy knowing that my time was slipping by and my chances of being first in line to meet her family was disappearing. In deed, I was one of the last to arrive in her town, and by that time her family was inundated with so many young people I was just another face in the crowd. It took a few more years to earn their attention. But, over the years, I captured the desire of Liz's heart. I did it through determination – doing anything to be near her, to win her (and her family) over. I wrote poetry, sang songs, gave gifts, sacrificed time, and energy, and money to win her over. She finally turned her desire toward me and made public declaration of that desire through her marriage vows. Now that we have been married for over 30 years, I am jealous to keep her desire. In many greater ways God has sacrificed everything to win us over - to be near us. He created us, loved us, saved us, called us, equipped us, and gave us gifts. He visited us. He lived, died, rose, and ascended to capture the desire of our hearts. He has done everything that is needed to win us over.

We merely respond by turning our desire toward Him or not. And He is jealous for that desire.

EVERYTHING WE NEED

The apostle Peter wrote, *"His divine power has given us everything we need for life and godliness through our knowledge of him who called us by his own glory and goodness. Through these he has given us his very great and precious promises, so that through them you may participate in the divine nature and escape the corruption in the world caused by evil desires"* (2 Peter 1:3, 4 NIV). God has given us everything we need to turn our desire toward Him. He has especially given us His Holy Spirit who lives in our hearts and guides us towards God's desires and away from "evil desires". This is **"the Spirit whom He placed in us"** (4:5). The Holy Spirit resides in the hearts of all those who put their faith in Christ. The main job of the Spirit is to guide us into discerning between what is right and good, and what is not. Jesus said, *"When he, the Spirit of truth, comes, he will guide you into all truth. He will not speak on his own; he will speak only what he hears, and he will tell you what is yet to come. He will bring glory to me by taking from what is mine and making it known to you. All that belongs to the Father is mine. That is why I said the Spirit will take from what is mine and make it known to you"* (John 16:13-15 NIV).

The Holy Spirit guides us into understanding all that we need to know for life and faith. He speaks through the bible. As we read it, meditate on it, and memorize it the Spirit helps us know God's will through understanding, believing and applying what God has revealed in His written Word. The Holy Spirit also uses our God given conscience. He reminds us of what we naturally know is good and right. The Spirit also gives us a holy community of wise followers of Jesus who can help us know what is right and good. And the Holy Spirit speaks in our inner heart as we grow in the disciplines of paying attention to Him and discerning His voice from the voices of the "evil desires" of *"the cravings of sinful (humanity), the lust of (the) eyes and the boasting of what (a person) has and does"* (1 John 2:16 NIV).

UPSIDE DOWN LIVING

James says, **"But God gives us even more free gifts. God says, "I resist the arrogant, but show favor to the humble"** (4:6). Here he is quoting from passages like Proverbs 3:34. God is turning the world's desires on their heads. More properly, God is righting the upside-down desires of the world. The "arrogant" are actually loosing out, while the "humble" are actually winning! Everything is being turned right side up! *"So"* says James, **"Surrender to God. And like God, resist the arrogant enemy and it will leave you. Draw near to God and He will be near to you. Wash your wayward hands. Center your wayward hearts"** (4:7, 8). Center your hearts

179

desires on God, rather than the desires of the world and you will get in on this right side up new world God is making.

James continues describing this opposite way of being: **_"Grieve and mourn and weep. Turn crying into laughing and joy into mourning"_** (4:9). James is encouraging us to change our complaining about the empty desires we crave (which do not satisfy us anyways), into delightful desire and enjoyment of God. He is describing turning from empty "crying" about what we wish we had, into joyful "laughing" in gratitude for what God has provided, and turning from chasing empty "joy" in pursuit of worldly pleasures, into some seriousness "mourning" for what is lost when God is not the center of our desires. This is not sad asceticism. It's not about denying worldly pleasures. It's about putting them all in their proper place under the first love of God and then enjoying the pleasures of this world in the ways He designed them to be enjoyed. I remember a personal conversation with J.I. Packer during which he said, _"Not enjoying pleasure is a rejection of God's goodness"_. Pleasures can be appreciated as gifts when a heart is turned to God. Pleasures are often grasped at and found empty when a heart ignores God. James is talking about finding true delight in the true desires of our hearts, which only truly find satisfaction in God, which is what you were uniquely created for. This is part of the way we experience the truly right-side-up-ness God is inviting us into. James says, **_"Humble yourselves before the Lord and He will lift you up"_** (4:10). Though we try to lift ourselves up in so many ways, ultimately it is only God who will truly lift anyone up. Again, this is part of God's right-side-up living in the way of Jesus; though it seems upside down in this world: By choosing the lowest seat, we are invited into the throne room. By accepting the status of a bond slave, we are welcomed into the royal family. By embracing humility now we will be glorified one day. Actually, I think we either embrace humility now, or humiliation will embrace us soon enough. The Psalmist wrote, *"Before I was afflicted I went astray, but now I obey your word ... It was good for me to be afflicted so that I might learn your decrees"* (Ps. 119:67 / 71 NIV). These are the personal choices we make daily in living in the desire to live the Jesus way. It is not something we may impose on others.

NO JUDGING

James continues, ***"Friends, don't slander each other. For the one who condemns a brother or sister judgmentally, misuses the law. And when you misuse the law, you make yourself the law maker and judge"*** (4:11). Embracing humility is a choice, not something we need others to force on us. We don't need others to heap humiliating shame on us. We all walk around with enough personal shame, thank you very much! We don't need to judge one another. In fact it is quite popular to hear, *"Don't be so judgmental!"* Yet we all regularly live under such heavy judgmentalism. We live with secret self-condemnation, deep shame, and private fear of others condemning us. So we spend a lot of energy justifying ourselves –

to our selves and to others. But that is the opposite of the way of true Christian community. We are all equally under the judgment of God. *"For the LORD is our judge"* (Isaiah 33:22 NIV). The writer of Hebrews stated, *"For a man is destined to die once, and after that to face judgment"* (Heb. 9:27 NIV). The apostle John pictured our ultimate end before the judgment seat of God: *"Then I saw a great white throne and him who was seated on it. Earth and sky fled from his presence, and there was no place for them. And I saw the dead, great and small, standing before the throne, and books were opened. Another book was opened, which is the book of life. The dead were judged according to what they had done as recorded in the books"* (Rev. 20:11, 12 NIV). This is the ultimate and serious end of all of creation. The psalmist wrote, *"Our God comes and will not be silent; a fire devours before him, and around him a tempest rages. He summons the heavens above, and the earth, that he may judge his people: "Gather to me my consecrated ones, who made a covenant with me by sacrifice." And the heavens proclaim his righteousness, for God himself is judge"* (Psalm 50:3-6 NIV).

We all equally stand convicted by God's righteous assessment of our sinfulness, but also saved by His free gift of gracious forgiveness and adoption. That's why the apostle Paul wrote, *"Why do you judge your brother? Or why do you look down on your brother? For we will all stand before God's judgment seat"* (Romans 14:10 NIV). God is the one who will judge each of us. We have no business judging anyone. The apostle Paul refused to be judged or to be bothered about other's judgment of him. He wrote, *"I care very little if I am judged by you or by any human court; indeed, I do not even judge myself. My conscience is clear, but that does not make me innocent. It is the Lord who judges me. Therefore judge nothing before the appointed time; wait till the Lord comes. He will bring to light what is hidden in darkness and will expose the motives of men's hearts. At that time each will receive his praise from God"* (1Cor. 4:3- NIV).

But, most of us do not possess the confidence of Paul. We live under the terrible fear of the tyranny of people judging us. I think that's mostly because we are so judgmental of others. We may not say them out loud, but we harbor many deep judgments about others. We might even believe it is OK to judge people's behavior. Many people act as if they believe that Christianity is all about obeying a bunch of religious rules and judging those who don't measure up to those behaviors. Meanwhile, there is common agreement that, while we have an obligation to judge other's behavior, people's religious experiences are private affairs and ought not to be questioned. This is a picture of much of contemporary Christianity: It is a practice of judgment and opinion, rather than grace and truth. Judgment and opinion says that we may judge another's moral behavior, but not their religious beliefs or experiences. We measure people's behavior, but believe everyone is entitled to their own private truth of God based on their own sentiments and experience. And experience tends to trump everything!

The way of Jesus is the opposite of these things. Jesus was full of grace and truth. The apostle John makes this point when he described Jesus (the visible image of God): *"The Word became flesh and made his dwelling among us. We have seen his glory, the glory of the One and Only, who came from the Father, full of grace and truth"* (John 1:14 NIV). Jesus was full of grace and truth. "Grace" and "truth" are the English translations of the two Greek words (*charis* and *aletheia*). These two words are the Greek forms of the two Hebrew words (*chesed* and *emet*) which the Psalmist uses for the very nature of God: *"Righteousness and justice are the foundation of your throne; love (chesed / charis / grace) and faithfulness (emet / aletheia / truth) go before you"* Psalm 89:14 NIV). Jesus was full of grace and truth, not judgment and opinion. The way of Jesus is grace and truth, not judgment and opinion. Grace is God's absolutely free and full gift of acceptance no matter what your moral performance is. Truth is the understanding of God's revealed reality. Grace and truth are cultivated through soft hearts and critical minds. Judgment and opinion is cultivated through critical hearts and soft minds.

James must have been thinking again about Jesus' Sermon on the Mount as he was writing these things to his scattered flock about judgment and opinion. The last part of that Sermon (Matthew 7) breaks nicely into two parts: The dangers of living by judgment (1-14), and The dangers of living by opinion (15-23). This is followed by a little, commonly misunderstood parable as a summary of the whole sermon.

THE TYRANY OF LIVING BY JUDGMENT

In Matthew 7:1-14, Jesus was making the point that there are several problems with living by judgment instead of grace (condemning one another's behavior) we will experience several awful results. Firstly, we are probably worse. Jesus said, *"Do not judge, or you too will be judged. For in the same way you judge others, you will be judged, and with the measure you use, it will be measured to you. "Why do you look at the speck of sawdust in your brother's eye and pay no attention to the plank in your own eye? How can you say to your brother, 'Let me take the speck out of your eye,' when all the time there is a plank in your own eye? You hypocrite, first take the plank out of your own eye, and then you will see clearly to remove the speck from your brother's eye"* (Matthew 7:1-5 NIV). Ironically, what usually makes us most upset about other's behaviors is often the very traits we are ashamed of in ourselves. It is so often our own self-condemnation that we are heaping on others. The word Jesus uses for judgment here is *"krino"* which means to pass a condemning sentence upon someone. This is not discernment. It is condemnation. We project our self-condemnation on to others. The apostle Paul said, *"You, therefore, have no excuse, you who pass judgment on someone else, for at whatever point you judge the other, you are condemning yourself, because you who pass judgment do the same things*" (Rom. 2:1 NIV). Let's not be hypocrites. Let's allow the Holy Spirit of God to work on the planks in our eyes before we judge any specks in our companion's eyes.

Secondly, Jesus makes the point that if we live by judgment instead of grace we are tossing God's grace to pigs and dogs. Jesus said, "*Do not give dogs what is sacred; do not throw your pearls to pigs. If you do, they may trample them under their feet, and then turn and tear you to pieces*" (Matt. 7:6 NIV). Tossing God's grace out and living by judgment is just going to turn back on you and bite you. The apostle Paul likewise said, "*If you bite and devour one another, take care that you are not consumed by one another*" (Gal. 5:15 NIV). Most of us know this experience too well. Living under judgmental condemnation is a biting and bitter prospect with everyone ending up chewed up and spat out. That is the opposite of the way of Jesus. It is not your job to be the morality police. It's God's job to judge (Is. 33:22, Ps. 50:4, Rom. 2). It's the Holy Spirit's job to convict (John 16). It's Satan's job to complain (Job 1, Rev. 12:10). Your job is to love and honor everyone unconditionally.

Next, Jesus makes the point that if we live under judgment instead of grace we actually miss out on God's gifts. Jesus said, "*Ask and it will be given to you; seek and you will find; knock and the door will be opened to you. For everyone who asks receives; he who seeks finds; and to him who knocks, the door will be opened. "Which of you, if his son asks for bread, will give him a stone? Or if he asks for a fish, will give him a snake? If you, then, though you are evil, know how to give good gifts to your children, how much more will your Father in heaven give good gifts to those who ask him! So in everything, do to others what you would have them do to you, for this sums up the Law and the Prophets"* (Matt. 7:7-12 NIV). The way of grace (not judgment) actually sums up the whole law and the prophets. You can sum up the whole of God's Law as: *"Love the Lord your God with all your heart and with all your soul and with all your mind.' This is the first and greatest commandment. And the second is like it: 'Love your neighbor as yourself.' All the Law and the Prophets hang on these two commandments"* (Matt. 22:37-40 NIV). So, in everything you do, receive God's grace and pass it on to others. Isn't that what you ultimately wish they would do for you? Isn't that *"doing unto others what you would have them do unto you"*?

Finally, in this part of His Sermon on the Mount, Jesus makes the point that if we live by judgment instead of grace we fall off the narrow path of the very way of Jesus. He said, *"Enter through the narrow gate. For wide is the gate and broad is the road that leads to destruction, and many enter through it. But small is the gate and narrow the road that leads to life, and only a few find it"* (Matt. 7:13-14 NIV). If we live by judgment instead of grace we wander off the thin path of Jesus' life and freedom. We get distracted into the wide, lost territories of legalism and destruction. Living by judgmental rules, games, comparisons, competition and condemnations instead of grace ends in our own destructions. Grace starts small but opens up into a wide life of freedom. We need to get away from the tyranny of religious performance. The only cure for living by the tyranny of religious performance is living by grace - receiving and giving grace to one another

THE TYRANY OF LIVING BY OPINION

In Matthew 7:15-23, Jesus was making the point that there are several problems with living by opinion instead of truth (putting faith in sentimental feelings) we will experience several awful results. Firstly, we will be duped all the time. Jesus said, *"Watch out for false prophets. They come to you in sheep's clothing, but inwardly they are ferocious wolves"* (Matt. 7:15 NIV). Relying on our sentimental estimations will lead us to trust other's persuasive seductions. They may feel like sheep, but they are ferocious wolves that steal our faith in the revealed plain truth of God's Word. The apostle Paul wrote, *"Keep watch over yourselves and all the flock of which the Holy Spirit has made you overseers. Be shepherds of the church of God, which he bought with his own blood. I know that after I leave, savage wolves will come in among you and will not spare the flock. Even from your own number men will arise and distort the truth in order to draw away disciples after them. So be on your guard! Remember that for three years I never stopped warning each of you night and day with tears. "Now I commit you to God and to the word of his grace"* (Acts 20:28-32).

Secondly, Jesus makes the point that if we put our faith in people's opinions we will often get rotten fruit. He said, *"By their fruit you will recognize them. Do people pick grapes from thornbushes, or figs from thistles? Likewise every good tree bears good fruit, but a bad tree bears bad fruit. A good tree cannot bear bad fruit, and a bad tree cannot bear good fruit. Every tree that does not bear good fruit is cut down and thrown into the fire. Thus, by their fruit you will recognize them"* (Matt. 7:16-20 NIV). How do we know if something is the good and right? Test it! Question if it is God's revealed truth (the real goods) or just someone's sentimental opinion. The apostle John wrote, *"Dear friends, do not believe every spirit, but test the spirits to see whether they are from God, because many false prophets have gone out into the world"* (1John 4:1). See, it's not about what it looks like or feels like. It might be a wolf in sheep's clothing. The proper question is: Is it God's truth? Examine every opinion to see if it is the Word of God? Examine what kind of fruit it is. Is it God's Word or mere human opinion? Test it. It's not about how it looks or even what the results are. It's about which tree is it from?

Too often we test things merely with more opinions. We say, *"It looks good to me"*, or *"It felt good to me"*. The music felt good. The speaker was wearing a nice suit. He used very persuasive

189

words. She used very persuasive magic tricks that made me feel really good. So, it must be true! Likewise, we may merely look at results. If there are a lot of numbers (people, dollars, buildings) we think it must be good, right, and true. But, just because someone can fill a stadium doesn't mean it is good, right, or true. Likewise, we might merely sense that it meets a felt need. We tend to ask if something meets my felt desires. We need to discern if something is of eternal value. If we are picking from the wrong tree, the fruit will be rotten no matter how desirable it looks or feels. Sometimes we are distracted and impressed by crowds of converts. But we need to ask what people are being converted to. Throughout history crowds of people have been converted to lies while sometimes even calling it "*spiritual*". The apostle Paul warned' "*See to it that no one takes you captive through hollow and deceptive philosophy, which depends on human tradition and the basic principles of this world rather than on Christ*" (Col. 2:8 NIV).

The next part of Jesus Sermon on the Mount is one of the most sobering set of verses in the whole bible. Jesus said, "*Not everyone who says to me, 'Lord, Lord,' will enter the kingdom of heaven, but only he who does the will of my Father who is in heaven. Many will say to me on that day, 'Lord, Lord, did we not prophesy in your name, and in your name drive out demons and perform many miracles?' Then I will tell them plainly, 'I never knew you. Away from me, you evildoers!'*" (Matt. 7:21-23 NIV). I'm sure it looked desirable, and very convincing judgment and opinion - but it was "evil". We need to get away from the tyranny of living by people's sentimental opinions. The only cure for the tyranny of living by people's sentimental opinions is living by truth; desiring, listening to, and speaking truth to one another.

DESIRING GRACE AND TRUTH

When God appeared in the flesh the apostles saw Him, and He was full of grace and truth. John said, *"The Word became flesh and made his dwelling among us. We have seen his glory, the glory of the One and Only, who came from the Father, full of grace and truth ... From the fullness of his grace we have all received one blessing after another. For the law was given through Moses; grace and truth came through Jesus Christ"* (John 1:14, 16, 17 NIV). Let's live in grace and truth. To live in grace and truth we have to truly desire it. We have to curb our natural desires for selfish powers, pleasures, and passivities. As we desire God's grace and truth in our lives, we can extend grace and truth to one another. With soft hearts and critical minds we can hold one another in the full love we receive from God. And, we can examine every opinion that comes along. Desiring grace means deciding to live under the free gift of absolute forgiveness and acceptance and not under the tyranny of having to perform for God or others. Desiring truth means deciding to live under clearly revealed Word of God and not under the tyranny of people's sentimental opinions about God.

Jesus' Sermon on the Mount ends with a little parable for <u>believers</u>: Jesus said, *"Therefore everyone who hears these words of mine and puts them into practice is like a wise man who built his house on the rock. The rain came down, the streams rose, and the winds blew and beat against that house; yet it did not fall, because it had its foundation on the rock. But every-one who hears these words of mine and does not put them into practice is like a foolish man who built his house on sand. The rain came down, the streams rose, and the winds blew and beat against that house, and it fell with a great crash"* (Matt. 7:24-27 NIV). Jesus is saying: *"If you hear this and do it (live by grace & truth), you'll be like a wise man who builds his house on a rock. But, if you try to live the Christian life by judgment and opinion, you're a fool with a house built on sand"*. Matthew tells us, *"When Jesus had finished saying these things, the crowds were amazed at his teaching, because he taught as one who had authority, and not as their teachers of the law"* (Matt. 7:28, 29 NIV). The teachers of the Law in Jesus day twisted the Word of God into a message of judgment and opinions. They were misusing the Law of God. That's not what the Law is for! James says, ***"There is only one Law Maker and Judge. He is the only one who can save or destroy. Who do you think you are to judge your neighbor?"*** (4:12). Let's desire the true grace and truth of God. Let's live into God's invitation to help each other live in grace and truth.

Let's pray

    Father in Heaven

You are so different from us

Let us experience Your Kingdom

of grace and truth

on Earth just like in Heaven

Give us today what we need

Forgive us and help us to forgive

Lead us away from desires other than You

Lead us away from the evil of judgment and opinion

Because it's all about Your Kingdom

Your power and Your glory, forever. Amen?

REFLECT:

Who do you conflict with the most?

How might God be jealous of your affection right now?

When have you experienced judgment?

When have you judged others?

When has someone's opinion let you down?

EXAMEN:

In quiet attention to God's loving presence, reflect on the challenges of desires.

In gratitude, when have you been strengthened by grace and truth?

How are you feeling about desires?

What is something about desires that you can talk to God about?

What is something about desires you can look forward to?

Seek God's guidance, help, and understanding. Pray for grace and truth.

EXERCISE:

Consider Jesus' question: *"What do you want me to do for you?"* (Mark 10:51)

Make a list of your desires. Look at the list and consider:

How many of these desires are for things?

How many are for personal pleasure, power, or achievements?

How many are for a change of circumstances?

How many are for character development?

Read Psalm 103, 145, and 37

Spend time praying for God's Holy Spirit to guide you into desiring God's priorities

Chapter 10

The Challenge of Security

James 4:13-18

Listen up, you guys, who so confidently say, "Today or tomorrow we're going to go to that city on the map where we're going to do some business for exactly a year. And we're going to make a load of cash". Oh, you are so arrogant and cocky. You don't even know what's going to happen tomorrow. Don't you know that you are really nothing but a puff of smoke? That's all your life is. You are here for a moment, and then you are completely gone. Poof! Instead, a proper attitude would be this: You should say, "If it's the Lord's will, we will live and do this or that". As it is, you are just bragging in your self-centered and self-confident self-promotion. All of this is such arrogance. It is empty. In fact, it's evil. The person who knows what's right and doesn't do it is knowingly doing wrong".

WRECKED PLANS

Can you think of a time when your plans got wrecked? In 1996, my home on the West coast of Canada experienced a dramatic winter storm. Any one who was living here at that time will get a glazed over look in their eyes if you mention "The Storm of '96". My city was shut down as record snow covered the whole community. No cars could travel on the roads. Medical staff were sequestered in hospitals for days. Any snowmobiles were commandeered by the police to transport emergency workers and patients. Many buildings collapsed under the weight of so much snow. Meanwhile, just as this mega storm hit, Liz and I, and our two young daughters traveled to Northern British Columbia to visit with my in-laws for Christmas. The day we left, we had to wait at our city airport for hours as all flights were delayed. When we finally got out of our city, we were trapped in the Vancouver International airport for another day. It was really bad. Our little girls did pretty well. They slept in a corner of the airport lounge covered by our jackets. But we had a harder time. It was physically and emotionally draining. People all around us were imploding with frustration as their Christmas plans were being ruined. We could see and feel people's crushing disappointment as they grieved missing precious family time. I spoke with a few people, and thought airports need to have pastors on hand for times like this. People were devastated and anxious and sad.

We finally got to our destination. But, we could not leave a week later as our whole Province was shuttered by the storm. We were stuck inside my in-laws' home for two weeks because it was 35 below zero! They are lovely people, but at that time they basically lived in one room. In this one space was the kitchen, connected to a TV sitting room. Throughout the two weeks we lived in that one space; Liz and I, our two young girls playing on the floor, all my in-laws, with a constant flow of visitors, people always cooking something, someone always on the phone, and the TV playing continuously. It was too cold to let our kids go outside for more than a few minutes at a time. I was going insane. We couldn't get out. We couldn't get away. I had a book with me that I really wanted to read. So, I just kept escaping to the washroom to get some relief from the chaos. My in-laws thought I was sick.

Our plans were wrecked. I hate when my plans get wrecked. I get disappointed and angry. I can get angry with God. I say, *"God, why have you destroyed my plans? God, what are you doing? If there is a God, why would He let this stuff happen to me?"* Don't we ask that sometimes? Don't we usually think that we are in control, and that our plans ought to work out the way we think they should, and that God must agree with us? We set our goals. We make our plans. And we organize the future as if nothing will change. But then things change, and we get disappointed, angry, and sad.

WE NEED A RESET

When we sent a youth team to Ecuador on a mission trip, their travel plans were disrupted by missed flights and lost passports. At one point we had members of our church youth spread over four countries. Some kids were stuck in an airport in a foreign country without an adult. Parents were very upset. On the Sunday morning of that week I received an email from the Youth Pastor who was on the trip. He gave me a message to pass on to our church. He said, *"Good morning everybody. And what a great morning it is. At this point, all eight of the remaining team members are on their way to San Jose, Costa Rica. Praise God. They had to find a way around that included going through Lima, Peru, but the team will be arriving in Quito (Ecuador) just after midnight tonight. They'll be picked up and taken to (reset) for the night."* He meant, "rest for the night". But I thought how profound. They were taken there to "reset" for the night. I think that's profound. I think that's what our next passage in James' letter is all about. It is about the "reset" that we need to make in our attitudes about our lives, and our plans, and where our true security lays. This is the invitation to examine where our securities truly lay; to test in what or in whom we have placed our security.

Authentic Christian faith requires real trust in God. Throughout the Scriptures we are instructed to "trust in God". A test of how firmly our faith is truly placed in God, is our reactions to those experiences when the plans we alternatively put our faith in get derailed. What,

200

or who do we actually put our faith in? Where do we actually find our sense of security? How about money? That's a tangible thing we often look to for security. Not many years ago, one could count on one's money doubling every seven years at a predictable 18% interest rate. One could know how much one had in RRSP's, and what one would have at retirement. But then a crash happened. There is a "correction" in the economy. Suddenly one realizes that nothing is predictable. Now I have to work 'til I'm 90 to have half the money I thought I would have!

A lot of us put faith in our future financial security. Others spend a lot of money on having security systems for their homes, or computers, or businesses. Others spend a lot of time and energy securing healthy bodies. We think we can control life, and property, and the future. Well, then we get to James 4:13-17. And the Holy Spirit of God through this church leader, James, has something to say to us about that. He launches into this blistering assault on that kind of arrogance we have in thinking that we can control anything. In fact, James uses a word for arrogance (*kauchaomai*) to expose our false confidences in anything other than God. The NIV uses the word "boasting". Here's another happy accident when James' First Century Greek language sounds like the English meaning. *Kauchaomi* - Oh, my, how cocky am I! We live in such cocky arrogance if we think we can control the future. As if we can even control tomorrow!

Remember, this flows out of the context the exhortation that James is giving to his flock flowing out of verses 7 through 10 of James chapter 4. He said, *"Submit yourselves, then, to God. Resist the devil and he'll flee from you. Come near to God and he'll come near to you"* (4:7-8a NIV). This is this repentance language. The word "repent" (*metanoia*) literally means to "change your mind". Reset your mind! *"Wash your hands, you sinners. Purify your hearts, you double-minded. Grieve, mourn and wail. Change your laughter into mourning, your joy into gloom. Humble yourselves before the Lord, and he will lift you up"* (4:8b-10 NIV). James is describing this attitude that we need to "reset" to. *"Quit being so arrogant"*, he is saying. *"Quit being so cocky. Quit thinking that you have things under control. Repent! Reset! You don't lift yourself up. God lifts you up - if you are humble. God will reset us if we allow him to"*.

Thomas Kelly wrote, *"Guidance of life by the Light within is not exhausted as is too frequently supposed, in special leadings toward particular tasks. It begins first of all in a mass revision of our total reaction to the world. Worshipping in the light we become new creatures, making wholly new and astonishing responses to the entire outer setting of life. These responses are not reasoned out. They are, in large measure, spontaneous reactions of felt incompatibility between "the world's judgments of value and the Supreme Value we adore deep in the Center. There is a total Instruction as well as specific instructions from the Light within. The dynamic illumination from the deeper level is shed upon the judgments of the surface level. And lo, the "former things are passed away, behold, they are become new. Paradoxically, this total Instruction proceeds in two opposing directions at once. We are torn loose from earthly attachments and ambitions contemptus mundi. And we are quickened to a divine but painful concern for this world — amor mundi. He plucks the world out of our hearts, loosening the chains of attachment. And He hurls the world into our hearts, where we and He together carry it in infinitely tender love.*

The second half of the paradox is more readily accepted today than the first. For we fear it means world-withdrawal, world-flight. We fear a life of wallowing in ecstasies of spiritual sensuality while cries of a needy world go unheeded. And some pages of history seem to fortify our fears. But there is a sound and valid contemptus mundi which the Inner Light works within the utterly dedicated soul. Positions of prominence, eminences of social recognition which we once meant to attain—how puny and trifling they become! Our old ambitions and heroic dreams—what years we have wasted in feeding our own insatiable self-pride, when only His will truly matters! Our wealth and property, security now and in old age — upon what broken reeds have we leaned, when He is "the rock of our heart, and our portion forever!" [47]

---

[47] Thomas R. Kelly, *A Testament of Devotion*, (San Francisco: HarperCollins Pub., 1941), 19, 20.

In the following verses (4:13-17) James turns his attention on to the businessmen of his day, as an example of the self-conceit we all hold when we place our sense of security in anything other than God. We can all apply his blistering exhortation to face the test of security. James says, *"Listen up, you guys, who so confidently say, today or tomorrow we're going to go to that city, that city right there on the map. That's the one. And we're going to do some business there for exactly a year. And we're going to make a load of cash. Oh, you are so arrogant and cocky. You don't even know what's going to happen tomorrow. You don't know that you are really nothing but a puff of smoke. That's all you really are. That's all your life is. You are here for a moment, and then you are completely gone. Poof. Instead, a proper attitude would be this: You should say, if it's the Lord's will, we will live and do this or that. As it is, you are just arrogant, cocky, bragging in your self-centered and self-confident self-promotion. As it is, you are so cocky. You brag in self-promotion. All this is such arrogance. It is empty. In fact, it's evil. The person who knows what's right and doesn't do it is knowingly doing wrong"* (4:13-17).

Now, making plans is not a bad thing. James is not saying to not make any plans. Plans for the future are not wrong. RRSPs are not evil. But it is essential that we do not put our faith or our hope or our confidence in ourselves, our plans, our savings, our bodies, or abilities. These things are a vapor; a puff of smoke, just an exhaling of air. That's all they are. Our lives and everything in them are just so brief and temporary; a mist. We need to reset, don't we? See, the only thing we can count on is that one day we'll be dead, we'll be gone like a puff of smoke. So we better start living now as if the only things that are worth anything are the things that matter in eternity. That's a reset. That's a change of attitude. It's a change of mind. It's literally a repentance. The only authentic place for faith and hope is God in Christ.

Remember Jesus telling that parable in Luke 12? He told this parable about the ground of a certain rich man, which produced a good crop. And the man thought to him self, *"Oh, what am I going to do with all this crop I've grown? I have got no place to store it all"*. He said, *"I know what I'll do. I'm going to tear down my barns and build bigger ones, and I'll store all my grain and my goods there; and then I'll say to myself, you've got plenty of good things stored up for many years. Take life easy. Eat, drink, and be merry"*. But, God said to that man, *"You are a fool. In fact, tonight your life is over, and now you will get what you have prepared for yourself"*. And Jesus said, *"This is how it will be for anyone who stores up things for himself but is not rich towards God"*.

ETERNAL PERSPECTIVE

What is Jesus saying? Well, first, he is obviously making a point of putting everything into eternal perspective. And he says that, above all, we need to be rich in relationship to God. Now, it's easy to pass judgment on the arrogant businessmen that James was using as an example, or the self-centered farmer whom Jesus referred to. But, what about all the things we put our faith and our hope into rather than God? How do we each need to rethink and reset our true security? Let's take that test of security and examine what things we put our faith into: How about that education? You know, that education that is going to get you that good job. Maybe it's the job itself that's going to give you the life that you want. It's going to get you the money to have the nice life and the nice house and the nice car. It's all smoke! All of that is a vapor. Some people that have lived well and long enough can look back at life and say those things were a vapor. How about friends and family? You may believe that these friends and family are going to be here forever; they'll never let you down. But then they leave. They get sick. They move away. They die. People are all smoke. We are all a vapor. Or what about these bodies? Some people can be prouder of your bodies than I can be of mine. You've really looked after yourselves. But, you know, every body is going to wear out. They are each a puff of smoke. How about our own resources? You might say, "*It's my money or my talents or my luck*". They're all puffs of smoke. And some of you can see your life or the things that you have put faith and hope in just drifting away like a mist. You try to grab it, and it's gone. Putting faith in anything other than the mercy of God is simply foolish. And we're not meant to only put our faith in God during a crisis. Our very existence depends on the mercy of God. Our very next step, our very next breath, our vey next tomorrow depends absolutely on the mercy of God. We should say, *"If it's the Lord's will, we're going to live and do this or that"*. Everything is utterly dependent on him and his will.

Now, James is not introducing some kind of magic formula or some kind of mantra to use. For instance, he is not meaning for us to just preface every sentence with *"If it's the Lord's will"*. That would get annoying. It's also not a magic formula. Some might think that if they just tack that magic saying on to the end of something, then it will happen: *"Lord, we pray for that, if it's your will"*, and then, snap it will make it happen. It's not magic. It's an attitude shift. It's a reset. Really, it's a reconversion that we need to embrace every day, in every event, in every decision we make in our lives. It's a reminder that we are not in control at all, that in humility we have to see that our very existence is dependent on God for every moment, and we live in his will.

GOD'S WILL

The idea of "God's will" has garnered some strange ideas and teachings. They are all around us. Young people are especially interested in "God's will". They may say they are interested in securing God's will for their lives. But what they are usually meaning is that they want security in knowing whom they should marry, where they should live, and what job they should do. And they want a secure, magic answer for those questions. They think that this would be "knowing God's will". Actually, this is the arrogance of our worldly thinking. It's even one of the ways that we try to have personally controlled security in our lives. We want to find out this or that information, or some secret knowledge of the future, so that we can be confident and secure in making the right choices by having everything figured out. We even treat God like He is a resource for our agendas. We think, *"Okay, I'm kind of stuck. I'm not sure of the next decision to make."* So we go to God. We say, *"God, I would like this information please; what is your will on this?"* And if we believe we got an answer, we say, *"Thank you. I'm done with you. Now you go back to heaven, and I'll go back to confidently going about with me in control"*. Do you see how that's treating God like a convenient resource for my own agenda instead of serving Him as the living Lord, whose will we are living in?

We treat God like He is a ceremonial monarch, while we are each the actual government of our own lives. Canadians have a constitutional monarch. She is Elizabeth the Second. She lives far away in England. She is the sovereign of our lives and land, but she really doesn't have much to do with my every day life. We sing a song about her at the end of many public events. She looks so good on our money or in a picture on the wall; very pleasant, very proper. She is wonderful to pull out on special occasions. She comes out, cuts a ribbon, and says a speech. That's neat! But the actual government of the land is the Prime Minister. If Queen Elizabeth ever came and messed with our country, or our personal lives, we'd be very upset. She is the sovereign. She can do what she wants. We can't actually do anything in our country without her ultimate approval. But, that's all just ceremonial right? This is the way we treat God, isn't it? Oh, He's the sovereign. He's good to pull out on special occasions, especially Sundays when it's nice to sing some ceremonial songs about Him. He's the sovereign, but I'm the Prime Minister of my own life, right? And, if God ever starts messing with my life, doing this, not doing that, I get so angry. How dare He!? We need a reset, don't we? God is not just a constitutional sovereign. He is not just the picture on the wall. No. He is the Lord of everything. We need to start living that way, don't we?

I think the better question is not asking whom one should marry, where one should live, or what job one should do; it's rather, how one should marry, how one should live, and how one should do whatever job one is doing? And God has revealed very clearly in His holy scriptures what His will is for those things, if we would simply pay attention. If we would reset, repent, and put ourselves under His will to listen to what He has said for how to live, how to be married, how to do whatever job we're doing. Those are the kingdom questions: *"God, how should I live?"*
God's will is about a whole different way of thinking, of making decisions and planning our lives in a whole different way. This life

is not about satisfying our own self-centered pleasures. In fact, that's impossible, when you think about it. God has built life in such a way that we cannot be satisfied in this life ultimately. God has made it so we cannot be satisfied in this life completely. He has built it that way. Because we will not be satisfied until we see Him face-to-face and live with Him for eternity. That will be true security, and satisfaction.

Speaking about guidance, Hannah Whitall Smith wrote, *"But if, upon searching, you do not find in the Bible any directions upon your point of difficulty, or if the directions given do not reach into all the especial details of the case, then you must seek guidance in the other ways mentioned; and God will voice Himself to you either by conviction of your judgment, or by providential circumstances, or by a clear inward impression. And in all true guidance these four voices will necessarily harmonize, for God cannot say in one voice that which He contradicts in another . . . If either one of these tests fail, it is not safe to proceed, but you must wait in quiet trust until the Lord shows you the point of harmony, which He surely will, sooner or later, if it is His voice that is speaking. Anything, therefore, which is out of this divine harmony must be rejected as not from God. For we must never forget that Satan can make impressions upon our minds as well as the blessed Spirit of God, and in this matter of guidance it is especially necessary not to be ignorant of his devices."* [48]

---

[48] Hannah Whitall Smith, *The Christian's Secret of a Happy Life*, (New Jersey: Spire Books, Fleming H. Revell Co. 1942), 68, 69.

But we run after things that will satisfy us in this life, and we're disappointed when they don't give us the security we desire. We chase after those things. We think, *"If I could just find the right person to marry who satisfies my every need; if I could just find the perfect job in which I am fully satisfied; if I just find the perfect church, perfect home, perfect community"*. Those things don't exist. There is no perfect family. There is no perfect church. There is no perfect spouse. There is no security in these fantasies. They don't exist. They are a puff of smoke.

When we chase after the things of this world looking for security, we will constantly be disappointed. But we can find security in God right now. Whether we're married or not, whether we have a job or not, wherever we live, we need to admit that, in our arrogance, we wake up every day putting our faith and trust in anything but God. That's what James means by **"bragging in the glorification of yourself"** (4:16 NIV). We need a daily reset. We all need to daily confront the challenge of security. We need to look good and hard at what our faith and hope is truly in. Is it really in God or not? I confess that it's true that I brag and glorify myself. I need to repent, and change my mind every day. I need to repent of putting my faith and hope in anything other than the mercy of God in Christ Jesus, the Lord of heaven and earth. Do you? Let's consider what

211

our faith and hope are placed in. I think we all need a daily reset. We get to examine our hearts before our loving Lord; asking: *What am I arrogant about? Am I arrogant in my own will? Am I cocky about my will, my ability to control my life?* It's all smoke. *What is my confidence in? Is it in my resources and myself?* It's all smoke. *What does my life glorify? Does my life glorify my goals, my agenda, my will, and me?* Ah, it's all smoke. Is your faith and hope in the living God or in things that are just puffs of smoke?

Let's pray

> *Oh, that we would put our faith and hope in you, Lord. Not in ourselves in any way, not in anything of this world: People, places, or things. God, we confess that we have put our faith in many things, but those of us that trust you right now reset our minds to put our faith wholly in you. Lord, help us do it every day. Amen?*

REFLECT:

When has it felt like God has "let you down"?

What do you have control over in your life?

When has God lifted you up?

What is your confidence in?

What does your life glorify?

How might you need to "reset" your attitudes?

What has disappeared from your life like a puff of smoke?

EXAMEN:

In quiet attention to God's loving presence, reflect on the challenges of security.

In gratitude, when have you been strengthened by trust?

How are you feeling about security?

What is something about security that you can talk to God about?

What is something about security you can look forward to?

Seek God's guidance, help, and understanding. Pray for trust.

EXERCISE:

List the things that give you a sense of security.

Imagine each one being in God's strong hands

Pray for each one and say, "Your will be done."

Chapter 11

The Challenge of Money

<u>James 5:1-6</u>

Pay attention, those of you with abundant financial wealth. Prepare now for the grief that is coming your way. Consider all your stuff as being already rotted, rusted, and devoured. All your gold and silver is cankered and tarnished. Their corrosive poisons will ultimately testify against you and prove your error. Ultimately you will be consumed with your hoarded pile when it's all burned up in the end. Pay attention! All the wealth you have gained through exploiting others is testifying against you. The exploited one's cries have reached the Lord Almighty. You have had your fill of devouring life's luxuries and feeding your own selfish indulgences. You have prepared yourself for your own ultimate destruction, by exploiting and ruining vulnerable people, who could not stop you.

One of the greatest opportunities God offers us for putting faith into practice is in handling money. We worry about money a lot. We all do. Those without financial security spend so much time worrying about how to get it, and those with financial security spend so much time worrying about how to keep it. My friend Colin told me, *"When I was a poor student, I was a communist. Then, when I started working and got some money, I became a capitalist"*. Too often we put faith in the things of this world instead of God, especially things like financial security, whether we have it or not. I think it's one of the greatest tests of faith for North Americans. North American people, like me, don't like talking about it. But James talked about it, and I think that the people of his day had the same tests and temptations and trials that we do.

Ask yourself in what ways you may be putting faith in money instead of God. It's not about how much money you have. It's about your attitude towards it. Because life is fleeting, wealth is fleeting. Only God's loving purposes are eternal and meaningful. If everything is created by God and exists to glorify Him, then only what is invested in devotion to relating to God is of any real worth. Only His loving presence, and His Word and purposes for history and for eternity are what are ultimately meaningful. Any resources that pass through our hands, are ultimately meant to be passed on in worship of God. So, how we handle money is one of the greatest challenges of faith in this life. My friend Bob says, *"Money doesn't talk. It screams!"* How we handle the challenges and opportunities that money confronts us with will scream godliness or self-centeredness.

Someone else said, *"Money doesn't buy happiness, but it can sure rent it for a while"*. I don't think that's a godly attitude, but it describes a way of seeing money as a means to get us what we want. We all think we'd be a little better off with just a little more money. I was on a board of a small charitable organization. It seemed that we were always stressed about money. We worried about money. We prayed about money. We fought about money. At one point, a member arranged to develop a store of financial reserves to operate as contingency fund for the organization. At first we were so relieved that we had this "extra" money and now all our financial worries would be over. Then we began to have worse fights over what to do with all that money!

I'm not going to tell people how to spend their money. But I'm going to ask some questions: What's your attitude about the money you have? Where is your faith? Who or what is your faith in? If your financial security disappeared yesterday or disappears tomorrow, where does your daily bread come from? It doesn't come from your stock portfolio. It comes from God. Our basic prayer is: Give us today our daily bread. We look to God and put our faith in Him. That's the whole point - to have faith in God, not as an abstract theory for life, but as a deep, relational reality, walking in loving trust with our loving God through the real, daily trials of life.

James starts this section by quoting Jesus' Sermon on the Mount. He writes, ***"Pay attention, those of you with abundant financial wealth. Prepare now for the grief that is coming your way. Consider all your stuff as being already rotted, rusted, and devoured"*** (5:1, 2). Remember how Jesus put it: *"Do not store up for yourselves treasures on earth, where moth and rust destroy, and where thieves break in and steal. But store up for yourselves treasures in heaven, where moth and rust do not destroy, and where thieves do not break in and steal. For where your treasure is, there your heart will be also."* (Matt. 6:19-21 NIV)

"Prepare now" for the transitory nature of anything this side of heaven. Do not put your faith in any material stuff. Everything of the material world is destined to be destroyed eventually. The whole of creation will be reconciled and renewed in the resurrection (Rom. 8:19-23). But, nothing of your worldly material goods is going to make it through the death and resurrection of creation. You won't be taking any of your bank balance or property with you into eternity. What James and Jesus are talking about is all the extra wealth we have banked up that are hoping will make our lives good in the future. He uses the word, *"plouto"* meaning the *"excess"*, or *"abundance"*. It's whatever extra we have banked up, that we are putting faith in now, to sustain us later. James is saying, *"Get this straight now. Don't put any faith in that extra wealth"*. In fact, he is suggesting we say, *"Good-bye"* to it now. Have a little funeral in your heart for it all, and be done with it. Imagine that it has all disappeared right now, and then ask: Am I still a child of God? Does God still love me? Do I still have eternal life? Do I still possess everything I need to know, love, and serve God with my whole heart, soul, mind, and strength, and can I still love my neighbor as myself? Then go on and live as if all that is true.

WE ARE ALL RICH

We all struggle with money. Whether we are wealthy or poor, we struggle to keep a godly perspective on finances. One thing that bothers us all is that we all think we are somewhat "poor". This is because there is always someone we can point to who has more wealth than us. But, if you were born in North America, you won the lottery in the world. You are part of the minority of the wealthiest people in the world. A while ago, there were North Americans calling out the wealthy 1% in America. People were chanting, *"We're the 99!"* meaning, we are the poor 99%, while someone else is the 1% wealthy. At the time, I thought, the rest of the world could point at every one of those "99%" and say, *"We're the 90%"* because any North American may be part of the richest 10% on the planet. And those of you who have traveled the world know what I'm talking about. But we can be in our little bubble, and as long as we can point to somebody richer than us, we can say, *"Well, I'm not rich. I mean, look at that guy!"* But North Americans may be part of the 10% richest people on the planet now, and may actually be part of the .01% richest people in all of human history.

James gets even more severe. He says to anyone who puts faith in hoarded wealth, *"All your gold and silver are cankered and tarnished. Their corrosive poisons will ultimately testify against you and prove your error. Ultimately you will be consumed with your hoarded pile when it's all burned up in the end"* (5:3). The NIV has the same English word "corroded" there for two different Greek words. The first one is *"katioo"* which means "rusty". The second one is *"io"* which means, "poison". It poisons our hearts to put faith in any of the rusty stuff of this world, which is all destined for decay. The Psalmist wrote, *"Do not trust in extortion or take pride in stolen goods; though your riches increase, do not set your heart on them"* (Ps. 62:10 NIV). The apostle Paul wrote to his protégé Timothy, *"... godliness with contentment is great gain. For we brought nothing into the world, and we can take nothing out of it. But if we have food and clothing, we will be content with that. People who want to get rich fall into temptation and a trap and into many foolish and harmful desires that plunge men into ruin and destruction. For the love of money is a root of all kinds of evil. Some people, eager for money, have wandered from the faith and pierced themselves with many griefs"* (1 Tim. 6:6-10 NIV). Many people are entrapped by "many griefs". People are anxious and worried. Jesus also addressed this in His Sermon on the Mount when he said,

"I tell you, do not worry about your life, what you will eat or drink; or about your body, what you will wear. Is not life more important than food, and the body more important than clothes? Look at the birds of the air; they do not sow or reap or store away in barns, and yet your heavenly Father feeds them. Are you not much more valuable than they? Who of you by worrying can add a single hour to his life? And why do you worry about clothes? See how the lilies of the field grow. They do not labor or spin. Yet I tell you that not even Solomon in all his splendor was dressed like one of these. If that is how God clothes the grass of the field, which is here today and tomorrow is thrown into the fire, will he not much more clothe you, O you of little faith? So do not worry, saying, 'What shall we eat?' or 'What shall we drink?' or 'What shall we wear?' For the pagans run after all these things, and your heavenly Father knows that you need them. But seek first his kingdom and his righteousness, and all these things will be given to you as well. Therefore do not worry about tomorrow, for tomorrow will worry about itself. Each day has enough trouble of its own" (Matt. 6:25-34 NIV).

Whatever we treasure will be what our hearts and minds will be consumed with. Ultimately, what our minds and hearts are consumed with, consumes us. It's a simple test. What is your heart and mind consumed with – God or money? What are you storing up – treasures in heaven, or treasures on earth? Are you worried and anxious about money? James says that our money will "testify (*martyr*) against us". Put it to the test: How are you handling money? How we handle money will expose the truth about us. Whatever we are focused on is what our eyes are alighted on. It's what is lighting our whole lives. Is it God or money? Whatever is alighting our eyes will ultimately expose who, or what our true master is. In the Sermon on the Mount Jesus said, *"The eye is the lamp of the body. If your eyes are good, your whole body will be full of light. But if your eyes are bad, your whole body will be full of darkness. If then the light within you is darkness, how great is that darkness! "No one can serve two masters. Either he will hate the one and love the other, or he will be devoted to the one and despise the other. You cannot serve both God and Money"* (Matt. 6:22-24 NIV).

Ultimately, the good news is that the Spiritual wealth we possess in Christ is so much more valuable than any treasures the world possesses. A person who is aware of and alert to the loving presence and lasting promises of God is rich beyond anything the world has to offer no matter what their financial status. I have access to the priceless treasure of God's loving presence every at every moment. I have the incomparable resource of God's Holy Spirit's guidance and encouragement every day. I have the priceless wealth of being a part of a community of Jesus followers. I have the matchless riches of God's luxurious promises for today, and for eternity. What worldly billionaire knows anything of comparable value to these riches? No treasure in the world can compare to enjoying the loving presence of God. When we are alive to the abundant goodness, truth, and beauty of God in our lives we are rich beyond measure. Whatever worldly wealth we possess is so much less valuable than the precious treasures we have in Christ. All Christians, of every financial status, can humbly rejoice in the wealth we possess; the incomparable richness of knowing, loving, and serving God, and enjoying His rich blessings forever.

RESPONSIBILITY OF MONEY

James then addresses how the money we have is a responsibility from God to be used for justice. It is a test of whether we are investing the wealth God loans us for His justice purposes, or for our own selfish indulgence. He writes, ***"Pay attention! All the wealth you have gained through exploiting others is testifying against you. The exploited one's cries have reached the Lord Almighty. You have had your fill of devouring life's luxuries and feeding your own selfish indulgence"*** (5:4-5a). We have to admit that we in North America have so overindulged ourselves with "devouring life's luxuries". No culture in history has had the luxuries that we have. And yet it's never enough. We keep spending more and more on things that satisfy us less and less. We tend to spend 110% of whatever income we make. No culture in history has had the debt load that we have nationally and personally accumulated, because we can never be satisfied with worldly luxuries.

222

James continues, *"You have prepared yourself for your own ultimate destruction, by exploiting and ruining vulnerable people, who could not stop you"* (5:5b-6). This is a sobering indictment of our self-indulgence and exploitation of others. There are four lies about money that many people believe. They are: *I earned it. It's mine. I deserve it. I can do whatever I want with it.* The truths are: Everything we ever have is on loan from God. He owns it all. It is merely on loan to us. Many people work much harder than you, but get much less reward. You are responsible for what you do with the money God has lent you. We must ask ourselves whether we are squandering what God has loaned to us in this life on ourselves (selfish indulgence), or are we using the world's unfair systems for personal gain (that is exploitation), or are we investing it in His mission of justice and mercy? What might that look like in your life?

The great 18ᵗʰ Century evangelist, John Wesley had a personal discipline regarding money that he not only practiced, but also taught to his Methodist followers. He basically made as much money as he could, but he lived on as little as he could, and he gave the rest away. He started out earning very little, but he lived within his means, and gave generously. By the end of his life he was earning one of the highest salaries of anyone in his day. Yet, he continued to live on about as much as he had been as a young man, and he gave all the rest away. In his senior years he was personally paying the salaries of many Methodist ministers, as well as many effective social justice initiatives in England and North America in his day. One can sum up Wesley's approach as: 1. Make as much money as you can (as long as it is made ethically). 2. Live on as little as you can (as long as you provide for your family's needs). 3. Give the rest away.[49]

Another discipline is to give away ten percent of everything one ever makes, save another ten percent, and live on eighty percent. If this were practiced over a lifetime, an average North American person living this way would experience a very comfortable life, retire comfortably, and will have supported many Kingdom ministries over time. We tried to instill in our kids a disciplined approach toward money. When they were young we decided on a formula for giving them each an allowance. We based the amount of their monthly supply on their ages. Then, we had them divide their funds into four equal categories. One quarter was for quick spending on anything they wanted. Another quarter was to be added to their savings towards something they decided they wanted to purchase in the future. Another quarter was for long-term savings for their education. The final quarter was for their own giving to any charities of their choices. This was sometimes fun, and sometimes challenging for our kids. But they did gain a first hand experience in handling their funds in a wise and disciplined way.

---

[49] Charles Edward White, "What Wesley Practiced and Preached About Money," Christianity Today / Leadership Journal, Winter Quarter, 1987.

What will our attitude about money be? Will our attitude be: It's mine. I earned it. I deserve it. I can do whatever I want with it? God gave it to me. Well, maybe He did. But if He did, He gave it to you for His purposes, not yours. Any material wealth is merely passing through our hands, on its way to the great bon fire of the resurrection of all things. As it passes through our hands, we are responsible for how we use it all. God is warning us in His Word. James is saying it's an opportunity to know, love, and serve God not self. And we have got to ask ourselves, am I trusting God or am I trusting in my wealth? Am I using my money wisely? Am I being mature in how I spend my money? Am I investing the wealth God has loaned me, in His Kingdom purposes, for His Kingdom justice? Am I exploiting others, and participating in the injustice of this world?

There's a story of a man who was a bitter, old, rich man. He went to a rabbi to ask for help. He said, *"I'm so bitter of life. I have all the good stuff of life, but I am not satisfied"*. The rabbi took him to a window in his study and he said, *"Look outside here. What do you see?"* The man looked out the window and said, *"I see my community. I see my neighbors. I see children playing, work happening"*. Then the rabbi took him to the other side of his study and showed him a mirror. Then he asked him, *"What do you see?"* He said, *"I only see myself"*. Isn't it interesting, just a little bit of silver changes a pane of glass into a mirror? Just a little bit of silver can turn us from looking out to the world into just looking at ourselves.   Sometimes that's all it takes. What is your attitude toward the wealth and affluence you have? It's not bad to be rich. It's just harder to live by faith. Again, some of you would say, well, I don't mind that test. Give me a little more of that burden; I don't mind. But remember, *"You cannot serve both God and money"*. The psalmist wrote,

> Trust in him at all times, you people;
>
> pour out your hearts to him,
>
> for God is our refuge.
>
> Surely the lowborn are but a breath,
>
> the highborn are but a lie.
>
> If weighed on a balance, they are nothing;
>
> together they are only a breath.
>
> Do not trust in extortion
>
> or put vain hope in stolen goods;
>
> though your riches increase,
>
> do not set your heart on them.
>
> One thing God has spoken,
>
> two things I have heard:
>
> 'Power belongs to you, God,
>
> and with you, Lord, is unfailing love;'
>
> and, 'You reward everyone
>
> according to what they have done.'

Psalm 62:8-12 (NIV)

Let's pray.

Lord, we would pray with Proverbs 30. Two things I ask of you, oh, Lord. To not refuse me before I die. Keep falsehood and lies from me. Give me neither poverty nor riches, but give me only my daily bread. Otherwise, I may have too much and disown you and say, who is the Lord? Or I may become poor and steal and so dishonor the name of my God. Help us to invest our resources in serving You. Amen?

REFLECT:

How do you handle money?

Do you consider yourself rich, or poor, or somewhere in the middle?

What are the greatest dangers you face around money?

What is God's invitation to you and money?

What might be a new habit you might practice with money?

EXAMEN:

In quiet attention to God's loving presence, reflect on the challenges of money.

In gratitude, when have you been strengthened by generosity?

How are you feeling about money?

What is something about money that you can talk to God about?

What is something about money you can look forward to?

Seek God's guidance, help, and understanding. Pray for generosity.

EXERCISE:

Read and consider Wesley's idea of handling money (Appendix 4). Prayerfully ask God's Holy Spirit to speak to you about how you are handling money.

Chapter 12

The Challenge of Time

James 5:7-12

Until Jesus returns, you need to be patient. Think about how a farmer waits for the ground to slowly produce a precious harvest and how patiently he waits on the seasonal rains. Be patient and stand firm. The presence of the Lord is coming. Quit complaining about each other, because the real judge is right there at your door. Friends, for an example of patient endurance in the midst of suffering, consider the Old Testament prophets. They spoke with the authority of God. You know, we regard those who persevere to be blessed. You have heard of Job's perseverance through suffering and how his life turned out in the end. And you know how compassionate and merciful the Lord is. Be patient friends. Wait and stand firm. Because you know what? The Lord is coming near".

PATIENTLY WAITING

Everyone hates having to wait. Can you think of a time when you had a frustrating experience waiting? Everybody has a story about trying to be patient. When I think about being patient, I think about being a kid. And I think one of the hardest things when I was a kid was waiting for Christmas. In our home, the Sears Christmas catalogue would come in early November, just after Halloween. My mom would hide it on me, because she knew I would just devour the thing. And I would be obsessed over certain pages. I would see that they got a new G.I. Joe and I would circle it. I would stare at it every day after school. I just couldn't wait for that day when I'd get that new G.I. Joe. Of course, then I would get it, and it would always fall short of what I really hoped for; right? I would think it was going to fulfill all my dreams, and then I would get my brand new G.I. Joe, and he would break. His arm would come off, or I'd loose his gun. Tragic!

The New Testament writer, James is trying to help his people understand that they need to persevere in the authentic walk of Christian spirituality. And that walk is a journey of growing in wisdom and maturity. That wisdom and maturity is cultivated through life's opportune challenges. The next invitation to cultivate wise and mature faith that James turns to is the challenge of time. I remember a 'TIME' magazine article about time in the late 1980's. It said something like, "*People today talk about time the way starving people talk about food*". That is perhaps even more true over 30 years later. People say, "*I don't have enough time! I have no time!*" I always wonder, "*Do their hours have less minutes than mine? Do they not have 24 hours in a day like me? Are their weeks less than seven days?*" Of course they have the exact same amount of time that I have each hour, day, week, month, etc. But we are all different in how we invest our time, and what attitude we have towards that investment. Many people do not intentionally invest their time in purposeful attention to growth. Instead their time is wasted in useless pursuits.

One of my favorite books about managing one's time is Gordon MacDonald's 'Ordering Your Private World'. In his seventh chapter ("Recapturing My Time") he provides "MacDonald's Laws of Unseized Time". These are the minutes, hours, days, etc. that we do not "seize" with intentional purpose, those loose moments that are not invested in purposeful commitment. These four "Laws" are: 1. Unseized time flows toward my weaknesses, 2. Unseized time comes under the influence of dominant people in my world, 3. Unseized time surrenders to the demands of all emergencies, 4. Unseized time gets invested in things that gain public acclamation.[50] When our time is "unseized" it is often wasted. Rather than growing in wisdom and maturity, people waste time pursuing mindless and heartless activities. Like money, time is a valuable resource that

---

[50] Gordon MacDonald, *Ordering Your Private World* (Nashville: Oliver-Nelson Publishers, 1950), 74-79.

needs to be budgeted, spent wisely, invested shrewdly or it will disappear too quickly leaving one all the poorer. Wise and mature people invest their time well.

One important way time is invested well is in waiting. A sign of Spiritual maturity is patience in waiting. Being patient in real time is hard, especially in the midst of whatever suffering we may be facing right now. The root of the word "patience" comes from the Latin, "*pati*" which means: "to suffer". We are not reared to be patient, are we? We are not a patient culture, are we? From the time we're born, we're in a hurry. Even from before you were born, I'm sure somebody at some point said, *"I wish this baby would hurry up and come out!"* And we're in a hurry ever since. We get pushed out into this world, and immediately everything is in a hurry: *Hurry up and take a breath. Hurry up and suck. Hurry up and eat. Hurry up and burp. Hurry up and smile. Hurry up and roll over. Hurry up and sit up. Hurry up and walk. Hurry up and talk. Hurry up and get toilet-trained. Hurry up and go to school.*

And then, by the time we're in school, many of us start to figure out that the best things in life are always the next thing. And we wish it would just hurry up and come. We think real life is always that thing that's just out of reach. It's always the next thing. Real life! We think, *"Oh, I just can hardly wait until I get out of kindergarten, and then I can go to real school. That will be real life. And then I can hardly wait to get out of primary school. I can be with the big kids. Then I'll really be living. Then I can hardly wait to get out of elementary school. Then I'll be a teenager, and that is real life. I can hardly wait until I get into high school. That will be real life. I can hardly wait until I get out of high school. That will be real living. I can hardly to get a girlfriend or a boyfriend, and really live. I can hardly wait until I get into university. Then I can really live. Then I can hardly wait until the final exams are over. Then I can really enjoy real life".*

THE NEXT THING

And it keeps going. Many of us think, *"I can hardly wait until I move out. Then I can start to really live. I can hardly wait until I get a real job, and then I can really start to live. I can hardly wait until I get married or get that promotion or get that vacation or get that retirement. Then I'll really be living. And then I'll really be somebody. I'll really be happy".* If you live long and well enough, you know that none of those things really satisfies us, especially because (it's obvious, isn't it?) it's always the "next thing" that we think is going to be the thing that satisfies us. And we impatiently chase after it. We keep on looking for the next thing. And we're always in a hurry. We want everything to be in a hurry. We want our cars to be fast. We want our entertainment to be fast and diverse. We want our food to be fast and diverse and disposable. We want our relationships to be fast and diverse and disposable. We want our spiritual fixes to be instantaneous and diverse and

233

disposable and on demand. I actually saw a website once called "God on Demand". Interesting!

So many of us want everything instantly, don't we? People want to lose weight instantly. We want to get rich quick. We want to grow muscles instantly. We want to get healthy quick. We want to regrow hair instantly. Some people want to get rid of hair instantly. We want to get wise and mature quick. We want a quickie life. That's how many of us live our lives, isn't it? We need to admit that. It's how we're reared to live life right from the beginning. You have got to hurry: *Hurry up and pay off that student loan. Hurry up and buy that house. Hurry up and get the better job. Hurry up and get the better car. Hurry up! You have got to hurry up and climb the corporate ladder. Hurry up and have children. Hurry up and get those kids to smile and sit up and walk and talk and get toilet-trained and then off to school and then out of the house. Because then you have got to hurry up and pay off your house. You have got to build up that pension plan and hurry up and retire so you can hurry up and get old so you can hurry up and die!*

Is this "hurry up and get to the next thing" real life? Is that what life is really all about? Is that the perspective of the way that life was meant to be; always living to get through this present time, because we are impatiently trying to get to the next thing, hoping it's going to bring us true happiness? Isn't real life what happens along the way? Isn't real life what goes on in the in-between times? Life is not the arrival at the event. It's the journey getting there. The in-between time, while we're waiting, that's life. This is it. This is life. It's not about the past. That's gone. It's not about the future. It hasn't arrived yet. This is it. This present is all we have.

And yet we impatiently race through it.

Are we just living for the next thing, or are we fully living in the moment that we're in right now? Are we living to get everything that God has for us in this in-between time? How do we escape that frantic, meaningless rat race through life? We know that joy is found in living in real time. Real life and real joy are found in the waiting. It's not the next thing that's going to satisfy us. It's the eternal thing that is right here, right now in this present time, and which will last forever. God is using this present reality to prepare us for an eternal future. It's a not yet, but it's an already. It's an already, but a not yet. We are living in the present reality of the resurrected life of eternity right now. That is the promise we have in Jesus Christ. And one day it will be completely fulfilled. But this present reality is where God is preparing us, using this present time and these very present circumstances to prepare us for the not yet. But, more than any other culture that the world has ever produced we are this impatient culture; and so we get this voice coming to us, the Holy Spirit through the scriptures, through that old, loving Church leader, James. From so long ago, he is saying, *"Until Jesus returns, you need to be patient"* (5:7a). A measure of how wise and mature you are is how patient you are in living in this real present time.

A FARMER

James gives us three pictures to illustrate this idea. He gives us three provocative images to illustrate the spiritual discipline of waiting. The first image is a farmer. Imagine a picture of a man in overalls sitting at a kitchen table inside his cozy home. Maybe he's reading the newspaper, or chatting with someone on the phone, or he's tinkering with some object. You might be surprised of that picture of a farmer. You might think, *"Why isn't he outside working on his farm?"* Because, James says, ***"Think about how a farmer waits for the ground to slowly produce a precious harvest and how patiently he waits on the seasonal rains"*** (5:7b).

James wants us to reflect on the fact that a wise farmer has to patiently wait for nature to do its miraculous work. He must live in the reality of the present while always patiently planning for the future. He waits for the rains to do their work. In the area that James was writing in, the rains would come twice a year. God does His work – sending sun and rain and bugs. Meanwhile, the farmer has to do something. As he is waiting for the rains to do their work, he waits. He can't make the rains come any sooner or any later. He can't make them come at all, actually, and he can't make the seed grow. So he waits. He has to wait. And he doesn't sit impatiently waiting for the rains to come; staring at his package of seeds in frustration, like me staring at the Sears Christmas catalogue. Can you imagine a good farmer doing nothing but stare at his crop, impatiently saying, *"Come on! Hurry up! Oh, I can hardly wait! Because when the crop comes that will be really living"*? No! A good farmer had something to do in the waiting. He wasn't impatient. But he wasn't passive. He got prepared for the rains. While he's waiting for God and the rains to do their job, one of the things he has to do is to make and mend the tools that he needs to have ready for the harvest that comes after the rainy season. See, the harvest was going to happen. Whether he's ready or not, it's going to come. But, will he be ready when it comes? The wise farmer spends time at his kitchen table, in his smithy, in his workshop. He spends time, patiently making and mending the tools he needs. That's important waiting work; to make and mend tools, to be ready for what's coming. Because one day he is going to need those tools. He doesn't need them yet. The harvest hasn't come. But one day he will need them. And will he have the tools he needs when he need them?

As we live fully in the present and take the time needed to do the hard work of waiting patiently in this present time, we can be ready when we need to be. Though we want to rush through life to get to the next thing, it's what we learn by patiently waiting in the in-between time that's important. I was talking to a university student one time, and she was having some tough personal struggles.

She had just finished her second year of university. I suggested that this would be a perfect time for her to take a year out and go do something different. I said, *"You are struggling. Take a year out. You need something that will develop your inner life while you wait for God to develop you, and to make plain what direction you need to take in your education. Go get involved in something where you'll be helping people who are having a tougher life than you, and maybe you'll get some needed tools and perspective on your life".* And she said, *"But then I would get behind!"* I said, *"Get behind what?"* I mean, is life a race? If you think life is a race, go find somebody who has won the race and see what the prize was. It's not a race. It's life! And it's what you are doing in this present moment that is preparing you for the harvest of the wise and mature person God is cultivating you into. That is the important thing. And the twists and turns in the journey are the very ingredients that are vital in producing that wise and mature person that God wants for His Kingdom.

But we race through the week, trying to make it to the weekend, when we can "really live". Aren't we supposed to be living during the week too? We want to rush through the journey, but the journey itself is the point. It's going to be over fast enough. ***"Be patient and stand firm."*** (5:8a) James says, ***"The presence of the Lord is coming"*** (5:8b). It's coming! You can't make it come any faster. And it's what God wants to do in the present time; in the waiting that counts. The presence of God is drawing near. James says it's coming whether you are ready or not. Meanwhile, he says, **"Quit complaining about each other"** (5:9a). We are all on this journey towards wisdom and maturity together. We can wait for each other. Let's be a little more patient with each other. We all have enough self-condemnation. We don't need to worry about trying to live up to other's judgmental expectations. It's not a race. It's also not a contest. Let's quit comparing ourselves to others, and judging others. Someone said, *"Compare yourself to who you were yesterday, not who anybody else is today"*. *"Because,"* James says, **"The real judge is right there at your door"** (5:9b). Jesus is at the door. Are you ready for him? The harvest is coming fast enough. Are you ready for it? Maybe like the farmer, you need to be waiting, working on those tools that you need for the future, to be ready for the judge when He calls you to serve Him. He's going to lead you in to opportunities to serve Him. He's going to call you to speak for Him, and act for Him. Are you patiently waiting and developing the wise and mature tools you need for right now, and for when that harvest comes?

THE PROPHETS

The second picture that James gives us, as an example of the spiritual discipline of waiting, is the Old Testament prophets. He says, **"Friends, for an example of patient endurance in the midst of suffering, consider the Old Testament prophets. (Remember those guys?) They spoke with the authority of God"** (5:10). Those Old

239

Testament prophets persevered, didn't they? They didn't rush their lives or their messages, even though most of them were killed for proclaiming God's prophetic Word. They suffered. They suffered in the in-between time, as God was testing them in the refining fire of service. And God used their refining, not just for them personally, but also for us, thousands of years later. Here we are, nourished by the Word of God that came through those Old Testament prophets. We read and sing and pray and study the Word of God written by the Old Testament writers, who lived in their own in-between times. They weren't rushing. They were waiting; waiting on God. And they waited for the new Kingdom of God that they knew God had promised and would deliver.

The Old Testament prophets prophesied about Jesus himself, but they never got to see him. So was that in-between time that they lived and waited in a waste of time and energy? No! God was preparing them. God was using them, not just for their own personal fulfillment, their own personal growth, but also for the growth of His faith community, for His salvation history plan. We are so grateful today for the patience and the perseverance of those Old Testament prophets. Most of them never got to see any of their own prophecies fulfilled. But they lived with a patient perspective of God's perfect eternity right there and then, knowing that God was speaking through them directly in the in-between time that they lived in. And it was an already but not yet. Their message was primarily *"Get ready!"* Get ready, not just for that future event, but get ready right now, be ready, be God's ready people, right now for what he wants to do right now and in the future. Get ready! Be people who are being present to God. Be people who are letting God make and mend you into tools that He wants and needs for right now, and for what He will do next. Because God is calling us to respond to Him and serve Him and be His representatives right here and now. He wants to use us as His hands; His words and faces of love, with all the people that we're going to see today, and tomorrow, and the next day and the next minute, all through this week. Be alert. Be present. Be ready!

God is doing something amazing. He's about to do something amazing, and those prophecies, the messages of those Old Testament prophets, were fulfilled soon enough. Were they ready for it? Were the people ready for it? Some were. Some were ready when they saw God face to face in Jesus. And God is also fulfilling His prophetic Word right now. Are you ready for it? Are you ready for what God wants to do in and through us in this present time, tomorrow, and throughout this year and the next ten years? Are you waiting on God? Are you getting ready for what God wants to do in and through you today? Are you ready for it? You know how we tend to race through life as if there's no reality beyond our next temporary fix or thrill. James says there's a judgment coming. Are you ready for it?

We are blessed in the waiting and the suffering. Jesus reminded his listeners about this in His Sermon on the Mount when He said, *"Blessed are those who are persecuted because of righteousness, for theirs is the kingdom of heaven. Blessed are you when people insult you, persecute you and falsely say all kinds of evil against you because of me. Rejoice and be glad, because great is your reward in heaven, for in the same way they persecuted the prophets who were before you"* (Matt. 5:10-12 NIV).

JOB

The third picture James gives us is Job, that Old Testament character. He says, ***"You know, we regard those who persevere to be blessed. You have heard of Job's perseverance through suffering and how his life turned out in the end. And you know how compassionate and merciful the Lord is"*** (5:11). Job persevered through intense suffering. God allowed that suffering to occur, and Job was refined through it. We will all experience suffering. That is life. But we can trust our compassionate, merciful, loving God to use our natural suffering to make us more compassionate people who ready to be His loving servants for today and tomorrow.

Do you see the progression in James' examples of suffering? The farmer must suffer the waiting of seasons to see his crop come to fruition. The Old Testament Prophets suffered the waiting for their

Words to see fruition in history and human hearts. Job had to suffer intense, personal suffering. Maybe nobody suffered more than Job. But, even in that, God was bringing about something great. Job had a terrible time. How could he have any joy or faith or patience during that trial? I don't know. Remember how his friends gathered around him and tried to explain his suffering? God rebuked them for that. All of their attempts at explaining it or categorizing it failed. That's not what it's about. It's not about explaining it away. Job persevered in real time, waiting on the eternal God in whom he trusted. And Job lived in it, and he soaked up everything that God could use in that experience to prepare him for what God would do. That's what James wants us to pay attention to. You can read it for yourself in the book of 'Job' and see what God brought about. Maybe we won't suffer like Job, but we can learn from these progressive tests of waiting on God like the farmer, the Old Testament prophets, and Job. We experience these images in our own present reality, as we are each being prepared by God for what He wants to do in us and through us. Job waited on God and believed throughout the in-between time. Long before that goodness came later, he had to be patient. He had to persevere. He had to trust and hope in God.

We wait on God. It's not about seeing what we would hope would come about. We often don't see the evidence yet, but we wait in it. And God uses that in-between waiting time to get us ready. But I keep wanting to rush through the process. Don't you? I think, *"If I can just get through the next thing"*. But faith and life are not something you "get through". It's in the getting through that we live, that we learn, that we grow, and where we develop the wisdom and the patience and the gentleness and the joy and the wholeness and the holiness that we need to better know, love, and serve God now and tomorrow.

I learned a lesson about this when I was doing my doctoral studies. I was working on my thesis, and I put forward seven different proposals. You know, most people don't do that. They give one proposal, and they usually get it passed. I put seven different proposals forward. And every time I gave a proposal, I had this fantasy that my advisor was simply going to phone me, and say, *"James, this is fantastic! It's fully developed. It's all there. Your proposal is perfect. Don't even bother writing your dissertation. I'm mailing you the doctoral degree. It's done. I can't believe how smart you are"*. That was my fantasy. But imagine, six times I had this message from my advisor, *"Uh, yeah, well, this is interesting, but it's nowhere near what we need"*. I was crushed every single time. I just wanted it to be done. But I kept handing in these copious amounts of writing, and he kept sending them back, saying, *"Yeah, that's super, but, you know, do some more reading and do some more writing"*. That's what he said every single time. I started to think that he actually wasn't even reading anything I was sending him. Because every time he'd say, *"Yeah, that's neat. Do some more reading. Do some more writing"*. I mean, I read hundreds of books. I wrote thousands of pages! I didn't want to read or write anything more! But he didn't care. He really didn't. He really wasn't that interested in anything I was writing or reading. He was interested in what I was learning. He had no interest in any of the scholarly stuff that I was producing. He was only interested in what kind of scholar I was becoming. He was waiting for that scholar to emerge. I think God is the same way. He's interested in us, and He is waiting for that loving servant to emerge out of the waiting process we are in right now.

REAL ENDURANCE

How can we be patient? What gives us the strength to wait and endure in the in-between time right now? James encourages us. He says, *"Be patient friends. Wait and stand firm. Because you know what? The Lord is coming near"*. Jesus will return. We are waiting on that final event of history. But, He is also drawing near to us every day as we wait on Him. The Lord is near to us. He's right here with you. So don't grumble against each other, friends, or you are just going to be judged. Look, the judge is standing at the door. The Lord is full of compassion and mercy. We can trust that whatever present suffering we are waiting in, will bring about something great. And we have got to trust Him with that. Like that farmer living fully in the here and now, preparing for the harvest day, making the tools, mending those tools that he needs for the harvest time. Like the Old Testament prophets doing their part for what's to come, not just for themselves but also for the whole community. Like Job trusting God even when it looked hopeless. We can wait on God to prepare us for whatever harvest comes when Jesus returns or the harvest of what he wants to do through you tomorrow morning. Are you ready? Are you ready for it? Are you prepared? I have to say I'm not. That's why I'm still in it. I'm waiting on God. That's why I'm still in the school with Jesus. He's still preparing me. And I hope to be ready. Whatever He's going to do in and through me today, helps me to be ready for what I need to do for Him tomorrow, and the next year, and ten years from now, because during the ongoing process of living life in Christ, He is making us into the kind of tools that He can use right now, and in the future.

That "tool" making kind of waiting involves taking the time to especially be in personal bible reading and prayer with God. Susan Annette Muto wrote, "*Once we begin wisely allotting time for reading and reflection, wondering and writing, we shall soon notice the reward. Life becomes less pressured, Christ, not the clock on the wall, becomes the center of our lives. Amazingly, we seem to accomplish more because our energy is not siphoned into pockets of useless worry. What a joy it is to make time our servant instead of our becoming enslaved to time*". [51] Dietrich Bonhoeffer wrote, "*Since meditation on the Scriptures, prayer, and intercession are a*

---

[51] Susan Annette Muto, *Pathways of Spiritual Living*, (Garden City: Doubleday & Co. Inc., 1984), 97, 98.

service we owe and because the grace of God is found in this service, we should train ourselves to set apart a regular hour for it, as we do for every other service we perform. This is not "legalism"; it is orderliness and fidelity . . . We have a right to this time, even prior to the claims of other people, and we may insist upon having it as a completely undisturbed quiet time despite all external difficulties . . . Who can really be faithful in great things if he has not learned to be faithful in the things of daily life" [52]

Do you know the story of 'The Velveteen Rabbit'? It's the story of a stuffed toy bunny in a nursery room with a young boy. There's a part in the story when he is worried about what it means to be "real", and he decides to ask the 'Skin Horse' about it one day:

> *"The Skin Horse had lived in the nursery longer than any of the others. He was so old that his brown coat was bald in patches and showed the seams underneath. Most of the hairs of his tail had been pulled out to string bead necklaces. He was wise, for he had seen a long succession of mechanical toys arrive to boast and swagger and by and by, break their main springs and pass away. And he knew that they were only toys and would never turn into anything else, for nursery magic is very strange and wonderful, and only those playthings that are old and*

---

[52] Dietrich Bonhoeffer, *Life Together*, (New York: HarperCollins Pub., 1954), 87.

wise and experienced like the Skin Horse understand all about it. 'What's real,' asked the Rabbit one day, when they were lying side by side near the nursery fender before Nana came to tidy the room. 'Does it mean having things that buzz inside you and a stick-out handle?' 'Real isn't how you are made,' said the Skin Horse. 'It's a thing that happens to you when a child loves you for a long, long time. Not just to play with, but really loves you. Then you become real.' 'Does it hurt,' asked the Rabbit. 'Sometimes,' said the Skin Horse, for he was always truthful. 'When you are real, you don't mind being hurt.' 'Does it happen at once, like being wound up,' he asked, 'or bit by bit?' 'No, no, it doesn't happen all at once,' said the Skin Horse. 'You become, and it takes a long time. That's why it doesn't happen often to people who break easily or who have sharp edges or who have to be carefully kept. Generally by the time you are real, most of your hair has been rubbed off. And your eyes drop out and you get loose joints and very shabby. But these things don't matter at all, because once you are real, you can't be ugly except to those people who don't understand.' 'I suppose you are real,' said the Rabbit. And then he wished he hasn't said it, because he thought maybe the Skin Horse might be sensitive." "But the Skin Horse only smiled.

'The boy's uncle made me real,' he said. 'And that was a great many years ago, but once you are real, you can't become unreal again. It lasts for always.' 'Oh,' the Rabbit sighed. He thought it would be a long time before this magic called 'real' happened to him. He longed to become real, to know what it felt like, and yet the idea of growing shabby and losing his eyes and whiskers was rather sad. He wished he could become it without these uncomfortable things happening to him." [53]

We know that it takes some uncomfortable things happening to us to make us the real servants of God He wants to make us into. We can hear the voice of Jesus saying, *"I especially love you. I am especially fond of you. So much, I want to make you real"*. We can live the solid life right now as we wait for God to prepare us to be ready for the harvest that is coming. That harvest will be whatever God might call you into as His representative in your neighborhood. So are you ready? Or is there more that God needs to work on? He wants to make us real. He wants to make and mend the tools that we need and the tools that we need to be. So are we ready? James says, **"Look it, above all, friends, don't make an oath by heaven or earth. Don't make that kind of promise. However, with anything else, just let your "yes" be "yes" and your "no" be "no" or you are just going to experience condemnation"** (5:12). Again, James is

---

[53] Margery Williams, *The Velveteen Rabbit*, (UK: George H. Doran Co.,1922).

quoting from Jesus' Sermon on the Mount. Jesus said, "*... you have heard that it was said to the people long ago, 'Do not break your oath, but keep the oaths you have made to the Lord.' But I tell you, Do not swear at all: either by heaven, for it is God's throne; or by the earth, for it is his footstool; or by Jerusalem, for it is the city of the Great King. And do not swear by your head, for you cannot make even one hair white or black. Simply let your 'Yes' be 'Yes,' and your 'No,' 'No'; anything beyond this comes from the evil one*" (Matt. 5:33-37 NIV).

See, "maybes" bring condemnation. Our feet need to be planted fully in the reality of living in the present. Be somebody who doesn't compromise. Let our yes's be "*Yes!*" and our no's be "*No!*" And with a perspective of eternal future, living fully in the present, making the most of the present -- letting God make and mend us, making us real right now. Right now is where we get prepared. Are you ready? Are you ready for the harvest that God wants to do today, tomorrow, and this year and ultimately when we see him face to face? Are you ready? Let's be patient. God is not done with us yet. Let's be patient with ourselves. Let's be patient with each other. This is God's workshop. And he's making and mending us, isn't he?

Let's pray.

> *God, we're so grateful that You have*
> *revealed Yourself to us in Your Word.*
> *You have given us, not a program, but*

Your presence. And we thank You that You are here with us right now, no matter what we're facing. All of us will suffer. We have either just come out of suffering or we're in the middle of it, or we're about to head into it. So, God we pray that You would give us the faith and the trust to see You and trust You in this in-between time that You are using to make us ready for what You want to do in and through us tomorrow, the next day, this next year. God, make us patient. Forgive us for our impatience. Thank You for Your patient compassion and mercy. Help us to grow through the challenges of time. Amen?

REFLECT:

What might be some things you are rushing right now?

What areas of your life do you need to just be patient in?

What tools is God making or mending in your life?

What tools have I got now that I didn't have days or years ago?

How is time making you more "real"?

How might God be using time to invite you into something new?

What do I need to say "yes" or "no" to?

EXAMEN:

In quiet attention to God's loving presence, reflect on challenges of time.

In gratitude, when have you been strengthened by patience?

How are you feeling about time?

What is something about time that you can talk to God about?

What is something about time you can look forward to?

Seek God's guidance, help, and understanding. Pray for patience.

EXERCISE:

Taking time to write out your time priorities

Put them into your weekly calendar:

> God: prayer, bible reading, meditation, fellowship, service, sabbath
>
> Spouse, children, friends, neighbors
>
> Work, learn, rest, play

Chapter 13

The Challenge of Prayer

James 5:13-20

Is any one of you in trouble? They should pray. Is anybody happy? Let him sing songs of praise. Is any one of you sick? That one should call the elders of the church to pray for them. And they should apply comforting oil in the way of the Lord. The prayer offered in faith will make the sick person whole. The Lord is going to raise him up. If he has erred, he'll be put right. Therefore admit your errors to each other and pray for each other so that you may be whole. The prayer of a righteous person is powerful and effective. Elijah was a normal believer just like us, and he was a faithful praying person. He responded to God's word, crying out to God with all his heart in every real-life circumstance. God proclaimed no rain through him, and Elijah kept praying. Then, three and a half years later, it rained again. Friends, if one of you wanders from the truth and someone brings that one back, remember this: whoever turns a wanderer from their errors will rescue that one from destruction and a lot of problems.

In the final part of his letter to his scattered flock, James focuses on the invitation to the challenges of prayer. He says, *"Is any one of you in trouble? They should pray. Is anybody happy? Let him sing songs of praise. Is any one of you sick? That one should call the elders of the church to pray over them"* (5:13, 14). He is saying that we need to pray in all of life's circumstances. He mentions three life circumstances, and directs us to be in prayer in each one. First he asks, *"Are you in trouble (kakopathei)?" (5:13)*. Kakopathei is the experience of bad circumstances. It's any *"caca"* in the *"path"*. Every human being experiences some caca along the way. The fact is that you are either in a bad experience right now, just coming out of one, or about to head into one. That's life! James means, *"If you have got any kind of trouble in your life, then pray"*.

The second life circumstance he refers to is *"if you have got happiness (euthumeo)"* (5:13). *Euthumeo* is to keep one's courage up; to be happy and cheerful. This is the opposite of being in frustrating "trouble". These are the good times between all the troubling caca. He says, *"If you have got any kind of happiness -- well, then, you should praise"* (5:13). And praise is a type of prayer. Prayer is always response language. We respond to the circumstances we find ourselves in. We may lament our troubles, ask for our needs, or express thanks for our good experiences. It's all prayer. So, James has covered the whole of life's circumstances (good times and bad). In all of it – pray!

Then, third, James asks, *"Is anybody sick (astheneo)?"* (5:13). *Astheneo* means to be weak. He means, if you are too weak to pray yourself – get others to pray for you. He says, *"Call on the elders (mature Christians who are wise in the ways of following Jesus) that they would pray for you"* (5:13). James is encouraging his friends to always be in prayer, in every life circumstance. And, if you're too weak to manage it yourself, call a mature friend to do it with you. We can turn to God in every life circumstance with prayer. That is what prayer is.

VITAL BREATH

Prayer is the vital breath of God's people. It is the very breath of our spiritual lives. But, there is much misunderstanding about prayer, so much misapplication when it comes to prayer. We need to review what prayer is, and what it isn't. Just to be controversial sometimes, I like to say, *"I don't believe in prayer"*. Let that sink in for a minute. I don't believe in prayer. I do believe in the God who listens to his praying people. I don't believe prayer itself has any power. I believe God is all-powerful, all-knowing, all-loving, and everywhere. God has revealed Himself to us, and He wants us to respond by faith, and the main way we respond is prayer. God lets circumstances happen in our lives, and no matter what those circumstances are we get to respond in prayer.

Now, of course, I believe in prayer. I believe we need to pray because prayer is the vital breath of the follower of Christ. But, prayer is not some magic formula that we can use to manipulate God to get Him to do stuff for us. Let me say this: The point of prayer is not to get God to do something for us. That is not the point of prayer. Unfortunately though, that is the most common practice of prayer through all of human history, and (most unfortunately) especially in the Church. The point of prayer is not to get God to do something for us. The point of prayer is that we would commune with the living God. The point is to engage with God, responding to His revelation, to his speaking, to his action in our lives in genuine, honest response, including lament, thanks, praise, and supplication.

How we pray is a test of what we really believe about God. I think the way that we pray actually demonstrates what we believe about God more than anything else. It's like the story of a guy riding his bicycle along a cliff. He falls, and ends up hanging by a branch over this cliff. He thinks, *"What can I do? I'm going to fall to my death!"* So he cries out, *"Is there anybody up there?"* And he hears the voice of God: *"I am here"*. The man asks, *"Can you help me?"* The voice says, *"Yes, I can help you"*. The man asks, *"What should I do?"* And God says, *"Trust me. Let go of the branch"*. The man thinks for a minute, then shouts, *"Is there anybody else up there?"*

This is just a silly story, and many people are desperately calling out, hoping there is "somebody else up there" who will rescue them from their circumstances. But, they may be missing the point of what prayer really is, and, in frustration, they may merely be erroneously using prayer as a means of getting what they want and wondering why God, if He exists, isn't giving it to them. And when God disappoints us, we wonder what use God and prayer is. We may not like it, but the point of prayer is not to get God to do what we want Him to do for us on our terms. And there is nobody else up there.

WHO ARE YOU PRAYING TO?

Maybe we need to change some of our ideas about who God is, how He operates, and what prayer is. C. S. Lewis wrote, *"The prayer preceding all prayers is "May it be the real I who speaks. May it be the real Thou that I speak to"*[54]. I mentioned these four key theological ideas about God; that He is all-knowing (omniscient), all-powerful (omnipotent), all-loving (omnibenevolent), and everywhere (omnipresent). These four ideas, held together, are the greatest challenge for people to understand the Christian faith. We look at our lives and it seems God can only be maybe two of those things at once. People wonder, if God is supposed to be all four of these things at once, how are we to make sense of suffering and evil? Orthodox Christian belief maintains that in some mysterious way,

---

[54] C. S. Lewis, *The Business of Heaven: Daily Readings from C. S. Lewis* (London: Houghton Mifflin Harcourt, 1984), 290.

God is all four of those things at once. Most people would say that this is impossible. The following may be the logical reasoning of the skeptic: *God can either be all-powerful and all-knowing, but not all loving, or not all-present. Because, if He was all-powerful and all-knowing, then He would do some things that He's not doing; so therefore He's not all-loving, or maybe just missing in action. Right? Or He can be all-powerful and all-loving, so He could do all things, and He does love us, so He wants to, but He's stupid or absent. He doesn't know enough, and that's why He's not doing what we want Him to do for us. As hard as we pray we can't get Him to do what we want Him to do for us. Therefore, I guess He's stupid. He would do it if He knew about it, but He obviously doesn't know about it. Or, God is all-knowing, really present, and all-loving, but He's obviously too weak to do anything about it. He knows what we need, and He loves us, and He really wishes He could do it, but He doesn't have the strength. Or, if He exists at all, He must simply just be absent.* Do you see that? Maybe this is where you are struggling with your faith right now. You are wondering how God can be all four of those things at once.

A WEAK GOD?

The way that we pray is a test of what we really believe about God. We demonstrate that we believe God is not all-powerful (omnipotent) when we pray like God is weak. We may pray like we believe God and his angels are kind of waiting in heaven for us to

259

give them the "authority" to act, like they are too weak to act until God's people pray. I don't find that idea anywhere in the Scriptures. I don't find God revealing Himself in that way. I think that's an idea of a weak God, and I don't believe God is weak. I don't think there's anything that is "binding" God, or that He needs to be "loosed" in any way. I'm using that language on purpose, because one of the misunderstood passages that people build their conception of a weak God from is Matthew 16. You remember when Jesus says to Peter, *"I will give you the keys to the kingdom of heaven; whatever you bind on earth will be bound in heaven, and whatever you loose on earth will be loosed in heaven"* (Matt. 16:19 NIV). If you only look at the English, well, no wonder you might be confused about that. Jesus was probably speaking Aramaic, but Matthew, by the Holy Spirit giving us revelation from God, uses an expression in the original Greek text that we don't use in proper English. There are double verbs. Jesus says, *"Whatever you bind* (aorist active subjunctive) *on earth will be* (third singular future indicative) *bound* (past perfect passive participle neuter singular nominative) *in heaven, and whatever you loose* (second singular aorist active subjunctive) *on earth will be* (third singular future indicative) *loosed* (perfect passive participle neuter singular nominative) *in heaven"*. In other words, *"Whatever you bind on earth will be what has already been bound in heaven, and whatever you loose on earth will be what has already been loosed in heaven"*. The fact is, we only loose and bind what God has already bound and loosed. That's what Jesus was saying to Peter. We have no power over God to get Him to do those things that He's too weak to do. That is an impossibility. We only believe, and proclaim, and do what God has already revealed. God is doing what He wants to do and what He has said to be true. He is the initiator. We are the recipients and responders. This is another test of prayer. Authentic Christian prayer is responsive, not initiating. But, again, the majority practice of prayer in the world demonstrates the erroneous concept of us coming to this inert God who is out there somewhere, who can't do anything until we show up and say, "God, I'm sure you are very glad I showed up because you are obviously too weak to do what we all know you should do. I loose you now to do what you have been holding off on doing". That practice of prayer demonstrates a conception of a weak God. It's not the biblical concept of God. He is all-powerful. We accept that by faith.

A STUPID GOD?

The next erroneous practice of prayer based on an erroneous idea of God, demonstrates a belief that God may be all-powerful, and all loving, but He is not all-knowing (omniscient); in fact, He's stupid. If we are honest, I think we all do this. This may be the majority kind of way that we practice prayer. We come to God and sometimes we are basically saying in our prayers, *"God, what's wrong with you? Don't you understand what's happening here? I can see it. Can't you? Are you blind? Are you stupid? How come you can't see what I can see? Because, I know you love us enough*

261

to do what we know is best, and you are powerful enough to do it, but you must just not be aware of it, so let me explain it to you." We find ourselves doing that in our prayers. But, as I said, God is the one who initiates. We are designed as response agents. It is God who created, not us. That's his first initiation, in our experience: that he created, that there is something, not nothing. And our basic response is either just to ignore it or to wonder and seek.

Secondly, it's God who has spoken, and we respond to what He says. As human beings, we have not determine for ourselves anything about the Spiritual realm. We can figure out all kinds of things. God has given us brains. God has given us reason to figure out all kinds of things about his creation. And we do that through the disciplines of history and science. But we can only figure out rudimentary things of the Spiritual realm through merely paying attention to creation. We have to wait for God to reveal it. And He does. He has spoken into our experience. He has told us news from the other realm, from the Spiritual realm, about what life is. And, again, we either respond by believing it (even if we don't fully understand it) or just kind of ignoring it. God has spoken in His Word. His Word is recorded for us in the scriptures. And, again, we can pay attention to it or just ignore it. And, finally of course, chronologically, the greatest and pinnacle of God's revelation is that He came. We didn't go anywhere to see Him. He arrived, and the person of Jesus Christ is the greatest and pinnacle revelation of who

God is. And, again, we can ignore that event in history or we can pay attention. We can respond by faith.

The other thing that we respond to is our circumstances. We find ourselves in whatever circumstances we are in at each moment. Sometimes find our selves clinging to cliff. Maybe you are that right now. You are in trouble, clinging to that wall. And God has revealed His Word to you, and you say, *"Well, that's not enough. Is there anybody else up there?"* Because it's not the answer I want. There isn't anybody else. There's only God, and we have to trust that He is all-loving, all-powerful, and all-knowing. But life happens to us, and we respond to our life circumstances, either in doubt, fear, despair, anger, or by faith. In fact, we respond in all those ways, and the great news is we can bring all those responses to God in prayer. Prayer is not trying to get God to do something for us. It's not trying to get stuff from God. Prayer is responding to the initiating God, with all of our fears and sadness and joy and celebration and anger and disappointment. Are you in trouble? Pray! Are you happy? Pray! Are you too weak to pray? Then call others to come and pray for you! God is not stupid. He knows exactly what's going on. In fact, He knows far more than you do about what's really going on.

It is a mystery why God allows events to happen to us. I sometimes wonder if God allows some crises to happen in our lives just to get us to respond to Him. We so often go through life ignoring God unless we are in crisis. Or is that just me? Some of us may have to admit that the last time you prayed was the last time you were in crisis. Well, maybe God is going to allow another crisis so that you will pray again, because that's the point. He wants to be in relationship with us, and he wants to be our loving parent. He wants us to commune with Him. Communing with God is about relating to the living God as our heavenly parent; as our master, as our friend, and prayer is our responding to that relationship.

A MEAN GOD?

And here's the other test of prayer. We may be demonstrating in our prayers that we honestly believe that God is all knowing, and all-powerful, but He is not all-loving (omnibenevolent). Do you demonstrate through your praying that you believe God is mean and capricious? Do you imagine that God does not actually want to give us what we need, and that we have got to somehow manipulate Him to do it? Do you pray as if God is up there with his arms folded, saying, *"Come on? What's wrong with you? Is that all the people you could gather tonight to pray? Well, I'm not going to do anything for you. Really? Is that your best effort? Let's see a few more tears!"* We know from his revelation that's not who God is. Why would we pray as if that's who God is? Maybe we think, *"If I was just a better person, God would love me more and give me more of what I want"*. But, there is nothing you can do to cause God to love you any more than He does right now, and there is nothing you can do to cause God to love you any less than He does right now.

AN ABSENT GOD?

Finally, we often pray in such a way that we are demonstrating that we really believe God is absent. There is even an ancient tradition at the beginning of Christian services when a leader will pray a prayer of "invocation". This may sound like we are trying to "invoke" God to show up. And perhaps that's actually what some ministers think they are doing. In reality, what needs invocation is our hearts and minds to be attuned to the fact of God's eternal presence – everywhere. Too many people think God only exists in special places, or only shows up when we summon Him with a magic prayer, or that He leaves the building at times. I hear people saying, *"Wow, God really showed up today!"*, or *"I think the Holy Spirit left"*. Of course, what they are really talking about is their subjective feelings. Maybe it feels like God is not there. Meanwhile, the psalmist wrote:

> *Where can I go from your Spirit?*
> *Where can I flee from your presence?*
> *If I go up to the heavens, you are there;*
> *if I make my bed in the depths, you are there.*
> *If I rise on the wings of the dawn,*
> *if I settle on the far side of the sea,*
> *even there your hand will guide me,*

your right hand will hold me fast.

If I say, "Surely the darkness will hide me

and the light become night around me,"

even the darkness will not be dark to you;

the night will shine like the day,

for darkness is as light to you.

Psalm 139:7-13 (NIV)

Likewise, Jesus made a promise to His disciples (and I think it extends to us) when He said, *"Surely I am with you always, to the very end of the age"* (Matt. 28:20 NIV). Jesus was promising that He would never abandon His flock. His Holy Spirit is with us and will never leave us or forsake us. God doesn't come and go. He is everywhere. He is omnipresent. Someone once said, *"If it feels like God isn't there, guess who moved"*.

IN THE LAP OF GOD

The God we meet in the Scriptures is our heavenly Father, and He wants to listen to us. The most helpful picture I know of, that helps me pray as if God is all-powerful, and all-knowing, and all-loving, is the image of being a child crawling up on to my heavenly Daddy's, or Mommy's lap and pouring out my whole heart to Him. I remember my own children getting on to my lap to speak to me. It was my favorite thing. I was so excited to have them share their hearts with me. And it didn't matter what the subject matter was. I just wanted to be with them and commune with their hearts. My son would crawl on to my lap and he would say something like, *"Hey Daddy, do you know that the capital of Canada is Ottawa?"* And, of course, any normal father would say, *"Oh brother! Come back when you have got something to tell me I don't know"*. No! Of course not!! I just want to commune with my son. Whatever he tells me is beautiful. I would say, *"Son, that's fantastic! What else can you tell me?"* Sure, I already know the information. It's not about him telling me things I don't know. It's about us communing. And I want him to come. And sometimes he would come up there and he would say, *"Daddy, I'm so afraid"*. I'd say, *"Oh, well then sit on my lap. Let's spend some time together"*. Or he'd say, *"Daddy, I'm not sure what to do. Daddy, I'm excited about this. Daddy, I'm hurting"*. No matter what it is, it's not really about that thing. It's about us being together. And I can care for him.

I want you to have that picture in your mind as you pray. Imagine crawling onto your Mommy's lap and bringing whatever is on your heart. We get to respond to the circumstances of our lives. We get to also respond to the things God has promised. We can confess and complain, praise and petition. We can say, *"Heavenly Daddy, I'm so afraid of this, or, God, I'm having trouble with this, but I know your word says this"*. We can bring all of that to him. God is all-loving, all-powerful, all knowing, and all present. He is our perfect Parent. The point is that He loves us and He wants to commune and communicate with us. He has spoken to us, and we respond in prayer, sharing all of our fears, joys, sadness, thanks, and desires. We also share with God our doubts, and confusions, and disappointments. Spanish philosopher Don Miguel Unamuno said, *"Those who believe they believe in God, but without passion in the heart, without anguish of mind, without uncertainty, without doubt, and even at times without despair, believe only in the idea of God, and not in God himself."*[55] Sometimes my children ask me for things, and sometimes I don't give them what they want. My son might say, *"Daddy, I really want a car"*. And I say, *"No. You cannot have a car. You are only twelve"*. It is not that I do not love my son. It is merely that it is not the right thing for him. And he may be very disappointed with me. He may not see things from my perspective. You know, the worst thing is when my children only treat me as an ATM. Right? They may only talk to me when they want something. I hate that! Well, it's the same thing with God. Often we treat God like our servant. Prayer is merely used to get God to do what I want Him to do for me, and I use whatever sort of magic formula I can use to get him to do it. We think, *"Boy, if I can just get the right number of people, if I can use the right posture, if I can do it this way, if I say the right word, God will give me what I want"*. In fact, we use *"in Jesus' name"* at the end like it's a magic word - like *"Shazam!"*

NOT MY WILL

---

[55] Quoted in Madeleine L'Engle, *Walking on Water* (Wheaton: Harold Shaw Pub., 1980), 32.

No matter how much effort or goodness or time we put into prayer, God is going to do his own will. And we need to pray according to his will, which we can know from his word. And when we don't know his will, we can say, *"Your will be done"*. Or when we don't like his will, as Jesus himself said, *"Not my will, but yours be done"* (Matt. 26:39). And Jesus, having that perfect relationship with his heavenly Father, came and spilled all of his fears, all of his apprehension, all of his feelings out, responding to the circumstances he was in. That's prayer. And God, the Father did not give Jesus what he wanted. God is not obliged to do whatever is not His will. One of the greatest questions that we have about the faith is why does God allow so much suffering in the world? I think it was G.K. Chesterton who said that the better question is why is there any goodness in the world? Why does God allow any pleasure in the world? Seriously, we don't ask that question enough. Sometimes in our prayers we think that God is obliged to do our will, and when he doesn't do it, we think He must be either not all-knowing, not all-loving, not all-powerful, or not all here. He's going to do what is His will, and He will never do what's contrary to His will. Well, then we ask, *"If He's not going to do what we ask for, then what is the point of praying?"* Again, the point of praying is not to get God to do stuff for us. The point of prayer is to commune, to have that relationship with the living God, our Father. We do not pray so that we get the stuff we want from God. We pray so that God can get the people He wants for His Kingdom.

But, of course, it's all about His will, and we are His servants, and prayer is a way that we respond to Him. As He is revealing his will to us, we respond. And you remember Jesus saying, *"If you remain in me and my words remain in you, ask whatever you wish, and it will be given you... the Father will give you whatever you ask in my name"* (John 15:7, 16). Of course to remain in me" and ask "in my name" is to pray according to His will, what He has already bound and loosed from heaven. We become sloppy in our prayers. We say, *"Prayer is effective".* But the reality is that it is God who is effective. Sometimes we say, *"God heard my prayer",* or *"God answered my prayer"* when what we usually really mean is: circumstances worked out the way I wanted them to. The reality is – God hears every prayer. God answers every prayer with His loving presence. And his loving children pray. So prayer is responding to his initiations, relating to the living, loving, leading God, surrendering to his will.

Though he may have never actually said these exact words, the script of the film, 'Shadowlands', has C.S. Lewis conversing with a clergy friend as his wife, Joy is battling of cancer. After hearing that there is good news about her prognosis, the friend says, *"God is hearing your prayer."* The C.S. Lewis character answers, *"That's not why I pray. I pray because I can't help myself. I pray because I'm helpless. I pray because the need flows out of me all the time - waking and sleeping. It doesn't change God- it changes me."* [56]

Again, we do not pray to change God's mind. We pray that God may change our minds, and everything else about us. We don't pray so that we can get the stuff we want from God. We pray so that God can get the people He wants for His Kingdom.

In her book, *'Clinging: The Experience of Prayer'*, Emilie Griffin wrote, *"Prayer is, after all, a very dangerous business. For all the benefits it offers of growing closer to God, it carries with it one great element of risk: the possibility of change. In prayer we open ourselves to the chance that God will do something with us that we had not intended. We yield to possibilities of intense perception, of seeing through human masks and the density of "things" to the very center of reality. This possibility excites us, but at the same time there is a fluttering in the stomach that goes with any dangerous adventure. We foresee a confrontation with the unknown, being hurt, being chased down. Don't we know for a fact that people who begin by "just praying" – with no particular aim in mind – wind up trudging off to missionary lands, entering monasteries, taking part in demonstrations, dedicating themselves to the poor and sick? To avoid this, sometimes we excuse ourselves from prayer by doing good works on a carefully controlled schedule. We volunteer for school committees, to be readers in church or youth counselors, doing good works in hopes that this will distract the Lord from asking us anything more difficult. By doing something specific and limited "for God," something we judge to be enough and more than*

---

[56] Shadowlands, directed by Richard Attenborough, 1993; DVD.

enough, we skirt the possibility that God—in prayer—may ask us
what he wants to ask, may suggest what we should do.

"Father, into your hands I entrust my spirit." Isn't that one of the
most disturbing sentences in the Scriptures? We know God asks us
hard things. We know he did not spare his own Son. We know Jesus
prayed, not now and then, but all the time. Isn't this what holds us
back—the knowledge of God's omnipotence, his unguessability, his
power, his right to ask an All of us, a perfect gift of self, a perfect act
of full surrender?"[57]

ANNOINTING AND HEALING

Let's continue our study of these final passages in James and point
out where some of the very words that James uses bring up some of
the very problems in people's ideas of prayer. You may even think
that James seems to be saying the opposite of all that I just said. In
the second half of 5:14, after James says, ***"Is any one of you sick?***
Call on the mature Christians who are wise in the ways of
following Jesus that they would pray for you" he says, ***"and they***
should apply medicinal oil on you in the way of the Lord" (5:14).
We have got to hear this in its original context and understand that
the application of oil at the time when James is writing was the
common medical practice. Oil was never a magic ointment. It was
never used as a little dab with a symbol to make a prayer more

[57] Emilie Griffin, *Clinging - The Experience of Prayer* (Wichita: Eighth Day Books, 2003), 2,3.

effective. No, it was medicinal. They would pour it over people. They didn't have a personal family doctor to go see. So, if they were too sick to pray, they could call a mature person from their church community to come visit. They may be the only people that really care about you. So they are going to come by to help you keep praying (keep being in that communal relationship with God), and also apply some medicine. James is prescribing prayer and medicine. I remember when a young man's appendix burst in our church. We all prayed, and we took him to the hospital. That's what James is saying. Using symbols in our prayer is great. A symbol of oil, that's great. But let's not confuse that with some kind of magic formula or something.

Now, it gets more confusing if we read the next bit in the NIV when James says, *"The prayer offered in faith will make the sick person well. The Lord is going to raise him up. If he sinned, he'll be forgiven. Therefore confess your sins to each other and pray for each other so that you may be healed, and the prayer of a righteous man is powerful and effective"* (5:15, 16 NIV). Is James saying that every time you pray for a sick person, they are going to get well, if you have got the right kind of faith formula or the right kind of righteousness? Again, this has led to all kinds of abuses. I can claim that I have healed you, because, you know, I'm powerful and effective and I claim that I have healed you, and then if you die, then I can simply say, *"Well, they stopped believing; it's their fault"*. It happens all the time. And people make a lot of money off of it.

273

That's not what James is talking about here. James means that prayer offered in faith – that is in trusting relationship with the living God -- will make a person right. The word he uses is *"sodzo"*. It means "saved", or "put right" in relationship with the living God, regardless of the degree of their continued physical brokenness. It does not mean that they will be physically healed. There is no promise of that in this passage. It means that this will help them stay actively on course with the vital discipline of being in that prayerful communion with God. If you are too sick to pray, get others to come and do the praying for you (and apply some medicine). And that kind of prayerful help in community will help restore you back into your relationship with the living God.

Sometimes God heals. Sometimes God will do miracles. As we bring our desires to God, we can tell him, *"God, this is what I want to have happen"*. And He will continue to do His will. He will do whatever His will is. It is not God's will to make everybody physically healthy all the time. We know we are all sick and dying. God allows sickness and death as part of his plan. But if we have faith in the living God through Christ, we will receive the gift of eternal life, and we will be raised from the dead when Jesus returns, and we receive new and perfect bodies then. These physical bodies will be resurrected, renewed. James says, *"The Lord will raise him up, and if he sinned, he'll be forgiven"* (5:15 NIV). God will raise all believers to eternal life on the day that Jesus returns, even if that person's sickness is because of sin, or if they have been too sick to keep in the communal disciplines of prayer. They will be raised if they are a believer in Christ.

LIKE ELIJAH

James continues, *"Therefore, confess your sins to each other, pray for each other so that you may be healed"* (5:16a NIV). That word *"healed"* literally means to be freed. It doesn't mean that one should expect to be made physically well. It means that one is free. Even if the sick person dies, they are free from this life of sin and sickness and death. They are spiritually free and have eternal life in Christ. Then James says, *"The prayer of a righteous man is powerful and effective"* (5:16b NIV). The prayers of righteous people are not "effective" in and of them selves. We have no power or righteousness of our own. As believers, we have the full righteousness of Christ; right standing with God through Christ. And prayer in the power of Jesus Christ is effective, because Jesus is effective and he is affecting the eternal and temporal lives of people every day.

Again, James may be misunderstood in the next part. He uses this example of Elijah, the Old Testament prophet, where he says, *"Elijah was a man just like us. He prayed earnestly that it wouldn't rain, and it did not rain on the land for three and a half years. Again he prayed, and the heavens gave rain, and the earth produced its crop"* (5:17, 18 NIV). It sounds like James is saying,

275

"If you would just be like Elijah, you'll have the magic powers to control the elements. If you have enough righteousness or enough faith, you can do miracles like Elijah!" It is interesting though; Elijah didn't have magic power to make it stop raining. He merely obeyed God's Word. James is quoting from 1 Kings 17:18, where we have this incident with Elijah and the rains. Now, what's interesting is that in 1 Kings 17:18, Elijah never prayed for the rains. He never prayed about the rains to stop or start. So that can't be what James means. James could have in fact used some other examples where Elijah did some pretty powerful things, like raising the widow's son, or what he did on Mount Carmel. Now that's a great story. These stories would better emphasized the idea that prayer is a magic power that we can possess if we have the right faith or formula. But instead, James uses this incident which emphasizes Elijah's practice of listening to God and praying to God and proclaiming what God had clearly said in his Word. It emphasizes Elijah's weakness, because Elijah didn't pray about the weather. God said, *"This is what I'm going to do. It's not going to rain."* So Elijah told them, this is what God said He's going to do. And then when it happened, Elijah ran away. When the rains stopped coming, he ran away and he hid, but he continued praying. In fact, one of the things he prayed for was that God would kill him and God said, *"No."*

So I think what James means is this: **"Elijah was a normal believer just like us, and he was a faithful praying person. He responded to**

276

God's word, crying out to God with all his heart in every real-life circumstance. God proclaimed no rain through him, and Elijah kept praying. Then, three and a half years later, it rained again, and all through it, Elijah kept praying. And his prayers were the life breath of his relationship with God" (5:17, 18). And I believe James has in mind the Hebrew way of prayer, which includes the holy habits of daily quiet time alone with God and fasting. But we are to do this in sincere relationship with our Heavenly Daddy, on His lap, not in some performance way. Remember what Jesus said in His Sermon on the Mount: *"And when you pray, do not be like the hypocrites, for they love to pray standing in the synagogues and on the street corners to be seen by men. I tell you the truth; they have received their reward in full. But when you pray, go into your room, close the door and pray to your Father, who is unseen. Then your Father, who sees what is done in secret, will reward you. And when you pray, do not keep on babbling like pagans, for they think they will be heard because of their many words. Do not be like them, for your Father knows what you need before you ask him. This, then, is how you should pray:* " *'Our Father in heaven, hallowed be your name, your kingdom come, your will be done on earth as it is in heaven. Give us today our daily bread. Forgive us our debts, as we also have forgiven our debtors. And lead us not into temptation, but deliver us from the evil one.' For if you forgive men when they sin against you, your heavenly Father will also forgive you. But if you do not forgive men their sins, your Father will not forgive your sins. When you fast, do not look somber as the hypocrites do, for they*

disfigure their faces to show men they are fasting. I tell you the
truth; they have received their reward in full. But when you fast, put
oil on your head and wash your face, so that it will not be obvious to
men that you are fasting, but only to your Father, who is unseen;
and your Father, who sees what is done in secret, will reward you"
(Matt. 6:5-18 NIV).

BRING IT BACK TO GOD

I have found that my prayer life is enhanced through disciplined
habits practiced over many years. One of y own habits is to pray
through the psalms each day. I "borrowed" the schedule of psalms
for ordinary days found in the front of an Anglican Church of
Canada prayer book. I crafted my own schedule from that as a guide
for using the psalms in daily meditation. These daily psalms are my
starting place for prayer each day. They get me started, especially
when my desire to pray is weak. They actually help cultivate my
desires to engage in prayer. E. M. Bounds wrote, *"Desire is not*
merely a simple wish; it is a deep seated craving; an intense longing
for attainment. In the realm of spiritual affairs, it is an important
adjunct to prayer. So important is it, that one might say, almost, that
desire is an absolute essential of prayer. Desire precedes prayer,
accompanies it, and is followed by it. Desire goes before prayer,
and by it, is created and intensified. Prayer is the oral expression of
desire. If prayer is asking God for something, then prayer must be
expressed. Prayer comes out into the open. Desire is silent. Prayer

is heard; desire, unheard. The deeper the desire, the stronger the prayer. Without desire, prayer is a meaningless mumble of words. Such perfunctory, formal praying, with no heart, no feeling, no real desire accompanying it, is to be shunned like a pestilence. Its exercise is a waste of precious time, and from it, no real blessing accrues. And yet even if it be discovered that desire is honestly absent, we should pray, anyway. We ought to pray. The "ought" comes in, in order that both desire and expression be cultivated. God's Word commands it. Our judgment tells us we ought to pray— to pray whether we feel like it or not—and not allow our feelings to determine our habits of prayer. In such circumstance, we ought to pray for desire to pray; for such a desire is God-given and heaven-born. We should pray for desire; then, when desire has been given, we should pray according to its dictates. Lack of spiritual desire should grieve us, and lead us to lament its absence, to seek earnestly for its bestowal, so that our praying, henceforth, should be an expression of "the soul's sincere desire."[58]

James ends his whole letter by saying, *"Friends, if one of you wanders from the truth and someone should bring you back, remember this, whoever turns a sinner from the error of his ways will save that one from death, cover over a multitude of sins"* (5:19, 20 NIV). Remember, he is addressing believers here. Sometimes we will wander away from authentic faith. We wander into all kinds

---

[58] E.M. Bounds, *The Necessity of Prayer* (San Bernardino: New Christian Classics Library, 2018), 21, 22.

of misbehavior. This is not about wandering from salvation. These people are saved people. But we wander away from the proper practice of the free life in Christ. And we easily slip back into any kinds of magic and manipulation, fear and doubt, neglecting vital daily habits of prayer. And we are responsible to help one another to stay on or come back to the way of a right relationship with the living God. That includes not treating God like He is stupid, or weak, or mean, or absent. This is especially true in our praying. Prayer is the life breath of Christians. It is a challenge. We demonstrate in our praying what we actually believe about God. Are you in trouble? Pray! If you are in trouble, let's lament and complain and confess. Are you happy? Let's respond to God in praise and thanksgiving. And if you are too tired, or sick, or fearful, or whatever to pray yourself, then call on others who are wise and mature in the faith to help you pray, to pray on your behalf, to do your praying for you. No matter what let's keep praying. And let's keep bringing each other back to God.

Let's pray,

Lord, teach us to pray! Amen?

REFLECT:

How is your prayer life?

What have been some helpful prayer resources for you?

What kind of God do your prayers show you believe in?

Who has brought you back to right relationship to God?

How might God be inviting you to pray?

EXAMEN:

In quiet attention to God's loving presence, reflect on the challenges of prayer.

In gratitude, when have you been strengthened by prayer?

How are you feeling about prayer?

What is something about prayer that you can talk to God about?

What is something about prayer you can look forward to?

Seek God's guidance, help, and understanding. Pray.

EXERCISE:

Spend time just sitting in your heavenly parent's lap.

Use the acronym "A.C.T.S." for prayer:

      Adore God in praise.

      Confess your sins and distractions to Him.

      Thank Him for all the truth, love, and goodness that you get to enjoy.

      Ask Him to **S**upply your needs.

Plan a prayer retreat – for a few hours, a day, or longer.

Pray the Psalms.

Use fasting (from food, or your phone, or TV, or whatever) to concentrate on prayer

Summary

I hope this study of James' epistle is helpful for you in understanding a little better what God may be saying to us through his servant James. We continue to face the challenging tests of trials, privileges, temptations, listening, discrimination, action, words, wisdom, desires, security, money, time, and prayer. This is certainly not an exhaustive topical list of all the challenges we face, but, I believe these are some of the things God challenges us with through James' letter.

REFLECT:

What other challenges would you add to James' list?

What challenges your faith the most?

What has helped you face and persevere through challenges?

EXAMEN:

In quiet attention to God's loving presence, reflect on these challenges.

In gratitude, when have you been strengthened through challenging tests?

How are you feeling about these challenges?

What is something about these challenges that you can talk to God about?

What is something about these challenges you can look forward to?

Seek God's guidance, help, and understanding. Pray.

EXERCISE:

Use what you have learned through this study to help others in their journey of faith.

APPENDIX ONE

Places where James may be directly quoting Jesus' 'Sermon on the Mount'

Sermon on the Mt	Themes	James passages
Matt. 5:1-12	Beatitudes	1:2, 2:5, 3:17-18, 5:9-10
Matt. 5:13-16	Salt & Light	3:17-18
Matt. 5:17-48	Fulfilling the Law	1:4, 2:10-12, 5:12
Matt. 6:1-4	Giving to needy	1:27
Matt. 6:5-15	Prayer	1:21
Matt. 6:16-18	Fasting	5:16-18
Matt. 6:19-24	Treasure in Heaven	5:1-2
Matt. 6:25-34	Do not worry	4:1-2, 5:3
Matt. 7:1-29	Judging others	1:5, 12, 17, 22, 2:4, 3:7-12,
4:2, 11-12, 5:9		

APPENDIX TWO

The Gospel of Matthew: The New Exodus

Exodus	Matthew	Theme
1:1-5,6:13-30	1:1-17	Genealogy
1:6-2:10	1:18-2:10	Infanticide
2:11-25	2:13-18	Fleeing from / Fleeing to Egypt
3/4	3:1-12	New Word from a bush / From a prophet
5:1-6:12	4:1-11	Pharaoh's trials / Satan's trials
7-10	4:12-17	Plagues in dark place / Preaching in Galilee
11/12	2:19-23	Passover / Jesus passed over
13-14	3:13-17	Red Sea / Jesus is baptized
15-17	4:23-25	Miracles in Desert / Miracles in Galilee
18	4:18-22	Appointing officials / Appointing apostles
19	5:1-12	Law on the Mountain / Sermon on the Mount
20:1-3	5:13	"One God" / "Salt of the earth"
20:4-6	5:14-16	"Idols" / "Light of the world"
20:7	5:33-37	"God's Name" / "Oaths"
20:8-11	17-20	"Sabbath" / "Law Fulfilled"
20:12	5:43-48	"Honoring Parents" / "Love your enemies"
20:13	5:21-26	"Murder" / "Murder"
20:14	5:27-32	"Adultery" / "Adultery"
20:15	5:38-42	"Theft" / "Give to the one who asks"
20:16	6:1-18	"Lies" / "Do not be like the hypocrites"
20:17	6:19-34	"Coveting" / "Treasure in Heaven"

APPENDIX THREE

My Translation

James 1:1-8

Hi! It's me, James, a servant of God and of the Lord Jesus Christ. I'm writing this letter to you, the twelve tribes scattered among the nations. Joy to you! Consider it pure joy, my friends whenever you encounter a multitude of trials of many colors. Because you know that the testing of your faith develops perseverance. Perseverance must continue towards its end goal that we may be mature and complete, lacking nothing. God doesn't want you to lack anything. So if any of you is lacking wisdom, for instance, you should ask God for it. And God, who generously provides wisdom to everyone, without finding fault, will give it to that person. The one who is doubting this is like an ocean wave; blown around, tossed by the wind. That kind of person isn't expecting anything from God. Anyone who doesn't trust God in the midst of these trials is double-minded.

James 1:9-12

Christian believers who are in modest circumstances should consider their privileges. Wealthy Christians should consider their humility. Circumstances are going to disappear like wild flowers. The sun comes up with scorching heat and withers them, and their blossoms fall and their beauty decays. Just like withering flowers, any possessions will disappear, even while they're being accumulated. When you persevere under life's challenges you are blessed, because when one has passed through a challenge, one will receive the ultimate reward of life which God has promised to those who love Him.

James 1:13-18

When one experiences temptation, one should not say, "God is tempting me". Because God is never tempted by evil, nor does God tempt anyone to do evil. One is tempted when one is captivated and seduced by a selfish desire. As one actively engages with that desire, a seed is conceived in one's life. That seed grows and is eventually born as a distraction from God. And, when that distraction grows up, it becomes death. Don't be deceived, friends. Every good and helpful thing we experience is a beam of light from God, the originator of all light, who never changes or hides in shadows. God chose to bring us to birth through His Word. We get to be the first fruits of all that God has created

James 1:19-27

My dear friends take note of this: Everyone should be quick to listen and slow to speak. Be slow to become angry. A human being's passion does not bring about the righteous life that God desires. Therefore, as you continue to get rid of whatever stuff that is keeping you from hearing God's life giving Word, and continue to throw off whatever superfluous stuff that is keeping you from running freely in this life, then you can humbly submit to the Word God has planted in you, which brings you to wholeness. Don't just listen to God's instructions and erroneously think you've got it. No, you've got to put it into practice for it to be real. Anyone who just listens to God's Word without putting it into practice, is like someone who that sees themself in the mirror, but forgets what they looks like as soon as they walk away from the mirror. The one who looks deeply into God's perfect, freedom giving revelation and does put it into practice, not forgetting what they have heard, but doing it will be blessed in the very practice of doing it. The Word of life, which we humbly submit to, that God has planted in you, which brings you to wholeness, blesses us as we practice living it. If anybody considers themselves to be truly religious, but doesn't keep their own mouth in check, only deceives themselves, and their religion is worthless. The true religion that our Heavenly Father God sees as pure and right is this: looking after orphans and widows in need, and keeping oneself from being distracted by the way of the world.

James 2:1-13

Friends, as the ones who trust in our exalted master, Jesus Christ, we don't discriminate between people. Imagine if one person shows up to your gathering wearing gold jewelry and nice clothes, and another person shows up wearing grubby clothes. If you give preferential treatment to the one wearing fine clothes, saying, "Here's a special seat for you" but say to the grubby one, "You stand over there" or "Sit on the floor by my feet" aren't you practicing discrimination and judgmentalism with evil intent? Pay attention, my dear friends. It's so like God to choose those who are insignificant in the world's perspective to be significant in the faith perspective, and to give them the riches of the Kingdom that He has promised those who love Him. But you discriminate against the poor, even though the rich (whom you exalt) are the very ones who are manipulating you. They're the ones who are exploiting you in the court system. They're the ones who are offending the integrity of the way of Jesus to whom you belong. If you are really keeping the way of the Kingdom found in bible ("Love your neighbor as yourself") you are getting it right. If you discriminate, you're getting it wrong, and you're condemning yourself. Keeping the Law, but missing this crucial bit is to miss the whole thing. For the one who commanded, "Do not commit adultery", also commanded, "Do not murder". If you do not commit adultery but you do commit murder, you are still a lawbreaker. Speak and act like those who live in way of grace that gives freedom, because discrimination without grace will be experienced by anyone who doesn't practice love and mercy. Mercy triumphs over discrimination.

James 2:14-26

What does it gain us friends, if we claim to believe but don't put our belief into practice? Imagine seeing your brother or sister naked or hungry. If you say them, "Go in peace. Be warm. Be fed", but you don't give them anything practical to supply their needs, what use is that? Likewise, faith alone without practical action is dead. But, someone might say, "You have faith, and I have actions". Try to show me faith without actions! Instead, I'll show you my faith through my actions. You believe there is one God. Well, that's good. But even demons believe that – and tremble! Do you want proof, you dummy, that faith without practical action is useless? How about old Abraham? Didn't he prove he believed when he offered up Isaac on the alter? Can you see that his faith and his practice worked together? His practice completed his faith. And, the Scripture says, "Abraham actively trusted God, and that proved his faith". And he was called "a friend of God". See? It's through practicing faith that one is called faithful, not just through believing alone. Likewise, wasn't Rahab, the prostitute called faithful because of her actions when she hid those spies and sent them safely off? She was called faithful because of her actions. Just like a body without breath is dead, so faith without practical actions is dead.

James 3:1-12

Let's not have many teachers, friends, because teachers will be most strictly judged. We all make mistakes. If anyone didn't make a mistake with their words, they would have already arrived, being in control of their whole life. When you put bits into horse's mouths, you can make them go anywhere you want. How about boats? They can be big, and they can be driven by mighty winds and waves, but with a little rudder pilots can steer them wherever they want. Likewise, tongues are a small part of any person, but they can make gigantic boasts. Think about how a destructive fire is started by a

*tiny spark. Human speech is a vicious gas leak ready to ignite. It's
a source of combustion within us. Sloppy words consume people's
whole lives. Corrupt teaching sets people's whole lives on fire.
Undisciplined speech spews burning smoke from the rotting local
garbage dump. All kinds of animals, birds, reptiles, and sea
creatures are being domesticated, and have been housebroken by
people, but no one can perfectly discipline their own mouth. Human
words can be poisonous, impatiently ready to speak error. With the
same mouth we can speak the good word to, or about our Lord and
Father, and with that same mouth speak a cutting curse upon other
people who are made in the likeness of God. Out of the same mouth
comes truth and lies, compliments and curses, heaven bound praise
and earth bound complaining. My friends, this is not right. Does
freshwater and salt water flow from the same source? Do fig trees
bear olives or grapevines bear figs? Likewise, a bitter salt source
cannot produce freshwater.*

James 3:13-18

*Who is wise and understanding among you? Let them show it by
living well and doing good work with gentleness that comes from
true wisdom. But, if you have bitterness and strife in your heart,
don't be boasting and lying. That kind of false wisdom is not from
above, but rather from below, and is merely worldly human opinion
and demonic lies. For wherever there is bitterness and strife, there's
confusion and every kind of evil practice. But, the wisdom that*

comes from above is firstly pure, then peaceful, gentle, rational, full

of mercy and good results, impartial and sincere. The results of this

kind of right living is flourishing peace.

James 4:1-12

Where do fights and strife come from? Don't they come from

conflicting desires that battle within you? You desire what you don't

have, so you kill. You're jealous because you don't have what you

want. You argue and fight and don't get your own way because you

don't ask. You demand but you're not satisfied because you look to

the wrong things to give you fulfillment. Don't you know that this is

adultery? That's because you are loving the world rather than God.

This makes God your enemy. Any one who lives to serve pleasure

becomes an enemy of God. Or do you think that Scripture is wrong

when it says God is jealous for the Spirit whom He placed in us?

But God gives us even more free gifts. God says, "I resist the

arrogant, but show favor to the humble". Surrender to God. And,

like God, resist the arrogant enemy and it will leave you. Draw near

to God and He will be near to you. Wash your wayward hands.

Centre your wayward hearts. Grieve and mourn and weep. Turn

crying into laughing and joy into mourning. Humble yourselves

before the Lord and He will lift you up. Friends, don't slander each

other. For the one who condemns a brother or sister judgmentally,

misuses the law. And when you misuse the law, you make yourself

the lawmaker and judge. There is only one Law Maker and Judge.

He is the only one who can save or destroy. Who do you think you are to judge your neighbor?

James 4:13-18

Listen up, you guys, who so confidently say, "Today or tomorrow we're going to go to that city on the map where we're going to do some business for exactly a year. And we're going to make a load of cash". Oh, you are so arrogant and cocky. You don't even know what's going to happen tomorrow. Don't you know that you are really nothing but a puff of smoke? That's all your life is. You are here for a moment, and then you are completely gone. Poof! Instead, a proper attitude would be this: You should say, "If it's the Lord's will, we will live and do this or that". As it is, you are just bragging in your self-centered and self-confident self-promotion. All of this is such arrogance. It is empty. In fact, it's evil. The person who knows what's right and doesn't do it is knowingly doing wrong".

James 5:1-6

Pay attention, those of you with abundant financial wealth. Prepare now for the grief that is coming your way. Consider all your stuff as being already rotted, rusted, and devoured. All your gold and silver is cankered and tarnished. Their corrosive poisons will ultimately testify against you and prove your error. Ultimately you will be consumed with your hoarded pile when it's all burned up in the end.

Pay attention! All the wealth you have gained through exploiting others is testifying against you. The exploited one's cries have reached the Lord Almighty. You have had your fill of devouring life's luxuries and feeding your own selfish indulgences. You have prepared yourself for your own ultimate destruction, by exploiting and ruining vulnerable people, who could not stop you.

James 5:7-12

Until Jesus returns, you need to be patient. Think about how a farmer waits for the ground to slowly produce a precious harvest and how patiently he waits on the seasonal rains. Be patient and stand firm. The presence of the Lord is coming. Quit complaining about each other, because the real judge is right there at your door. Friends, for an example of patient endurance in the midst of suffering, consider the Old Testament prophets. They spoke with the authority of God. You know, we regard those who persevere to be blessed. You have heard of Job's perseverance through suffering and how his life turned out in the end. And you know how compassionate and merciful the Lord is. Be patient friends. Wait and stand firm. Because you know what? The Lord is coming near".

James 5:13-20

Is any one of you in trouble? They should pray. Is anybody happy? Let him sing songs of praise. Is any one of you sick? That one should call the elders of the church to pray for them. And they should apply comforting oil in the way of the Lord. The prayer offered in faith will make the sick person whole. The Lord is going to raise him up. If he has erred, he'll be put right. Therefore admit your errors to each other and pray for each other so that you may be whole. The prayer of a righteous person is powerful and effective. Elijah was a normal believer just like us, and he was a faithful praying person. He responded to God's word, crying out to God with all his heart in every real-life circumstance. God proclaimed no rain through him, and Elijah kept praying. Then, three and a half years later, it rained again. Friends, if one of you wanders from the truth and someone brings that one back, remember this: whoever turns a wanderer from their errors will rescue that one from destruction and a lot of problems.

Made in the USA
San Bernardino, CA
19 April 2019